TOMORROW

The profound crisis affecting our societies is obvious. Ecological disturbances, social exclusion, the rampant exploitation of natural resources, the frenetic and dehumanizing quest for profit and the widening of inequalities lie at the heart of our contemporary problems.

Nevertheless, men and women everywhere are coming together around innovative and original projects with a view to opening up new prospects for the future. There are solutions. Novel proposals are being made all over the planet, often on a small scale, but always with the aim of bringing about real change in our societies.

THE POWER OF RESTRAINT

In the same series

Rob Hopkins and Lionel Astruc, *The Transition Starts Here, Now and Together*, 2017.
Cyril Dion, *Tomorrow*, 2017.
Lionel Astruc, *Vandana Shiva: Creative Civil Disobedience*, 2017.

Originally published in French as
Vers la sobriété heureuse, by Actes Sud in 2010.

© Actes Sud, 2017
ISBN 978-2-330-08126-3
www.actes-sud.fr

PIERRE RABHI

THE POWER OF RESTRAINT

Translated by Lisa Davidson

TOMORROW
ACTES SUD

The greatest, most beautiful accomplishment of our age will be to meet the basic needs of all humanity in simpler, healthier ways. Growing a garden or undertaking any activity that fosters autonomy will be viewed as a political act, an act of legitimate resistance against the dependence and enslavement of the individual.

PIERRE RABHI

PREFACE   10

1. THE SEEDS OF REBELLION   12
1. THE SONG OF THE BLACKSMITH   13
2. DISILLUSIONMENT   18
3. DECLINE OF RURAL LIFE   20

2. THE SHAM OF THE MODERN AGE   28
1. PROGRESS: BETWEEN MYTH AND REALITY   30
2. DOMINATION OF THE PROFIT MOTIVE   35
3. BREAKDOWN OF UNIVERSAL PRINCIPLES   40

3. RESTRAINT, AN ANCESTRAL WISDOM   46
1. AN AFRICAN VILLAGE   48
2. THE YEAR 1985   51
3. NOTHING IS LOST, NOTHING IS CREATED, EVERYTHING IS TRANSFORMED   54
4. CONNECTING WITH THE SACRED NATURE OF LIFE   61

4. IN SUPPORT OF RESTRAINT   64
1. POVERTY AS A MEASURE OF WELL-BEING   65
2. VOLUNTARY RESTRAINT   70
3. HUMAN CHANGE   75
4. A PLEA FOR CONSTRUCTIVE INDIGNATION   85

APPENDICES   90
1. BEAUTIFUL DREAMS, TO SCATTER FOR FUTURE GENERATIONS   91
2. INTERNATIONAL CHARTER FOR THE EARTH AND HUMANITY   92
3. LES AMANINS: CREATION OF AN ECOLOGICAL, EDUCATIONAL AND SOLIDARITY-BASED SITE   96
4. COLIBRIS: A PLATFORM FOR MEETINGS AND EXCHANGES   97
5. THE FERME DES ENFANTS AND THE HAMEAU DES BUIS: BUILDING THE FUTURE WITH A RESPECT FOR LIFE   100
6. THE SOLAN MONASTERY: COMBINING LITURGY AND FARMING   101
7. TERRE & HUMANISME: TRANSMITTING AGROECOLOGY HERE AND ELSEWHERE ...   103
8. OUTREACH AND PROSPECTS FOR THE FUTURE   104

PREFACE

For forty-five years, I have lived my life according to the precepts of restraint, with the support and cooperation of Michèle and our family. Rather than indulge in general theories or opinions, I would rather relate the series of insights, decisions, and initiatives that have been inspired by this conscious choice. By adhering to the principle, "Do what I say and say what I do," I hope to impart some coherence and credibility to my humble account. My sole ambition here is to contribute a few thoughts to inform decisions that cannot be forever deferred without serious consequences for the immediate future, and even more so in the medium and long term. Regardless of what you think about restraint as an inescapable necessity, one thing remains certain: the limits imposed by the very nature of planet earth render the principle of unlimited economic growth unrealistic and absurd–unrealistic, if we apply the most basic analytical tools, either physical or biological, to the phenomenon of life; absurd when examined through simple, clear-sighted logic. The dominant system prides itself on its excellent results, yet goes to great lengths to gloss over its inefficiency; this would become clear if a straightforward appraisal, notably concerning energy, were made. This assessment would also reveal the internal contradictions of a model that cannot produce without destroying and therefore carries within it the seeds of its own destruction. The time has come to establish an overarching policy based on the power of restraint. An exciting project lies ahead, calling on each and every one of us to work toward the greatest possible creative goal: meeting our essential needs in the simplest, healthiest way. This liberating option is a political act, an act of resistance against everything that, in the name of progress, is ruining the planet by alienating the individual. It is the beauty of nature, of life, and of the creative dimension of mankind that should constantly inspire us as we embark on new paths.

1

THE SEEDS OF REBELLION

1. The song of the blacksmith

A simple man, living in a small oasis in the south of Algeria, goes about his business as usual, providing for his family as best he can. He opens the door to his blacksmith's shop, lights the fire and works all day fashioning metal. He maintains the farmers' tools and repairs everyday objects. This small-scale desert Vulcan spends all day making his anvil sing, while an apprentice pulls on the rope of the forge bellows to fan the flames. Incandescent sparks leap off the hammer, forming a luminous cloud, while the blacksmith, totally concentrated on his work, seems to be in another world.

A quiet child watches him in admiration, immensely proud. From time to time, the lean, determined-looking man, dripping in sweat, stops, greets customers, answers their questions. Sometimes, a group of men forms spontaneously in front of the shop. They talk, drink tea, tell jokes, laugh, and also discuss serious issues, squatting on palm-fiber mats.

Not far from the workshop is a fairly large square, lined with shops—grocery stores, butchers, fabric stores, etc.—as well as tailors, shoemakers, carpenters, and goldsmiths. Every day, songs waft out of the workshops like small bits of serenity, spreading out into the air that is warm or stifling, depending on the season. An empty open space on the western edge is home to the market, a sort of open-air caravanserai with a rank-smelling tangle of grunting camels, sheep, goats, donkeys, and horses. Silent nomads come and go. Others stay, crouching against rough burlap bags stuffed with grain, their bundles of dry wood evoking images of the wide, open desert where they were gathered. Dates packed for long conservation and desert truffles, when in season, are available for sale. All this generates a kind of muffled chaos, interrupted by the sharp cries of merchants shouting out to customers. Storytellers and acrobats sometimes offer their skills and dreams to a fascinated public, gathered in a circle around them. The entire town consists of small alleys, winding through the shade of ocher-colored mud houses with rooftop terraces crammed side by side, surrounding a white minaret that looks like a watchman scanning the horizon line. A few palm trees emerge from this mass of clay. Some serve as parasols, offering shade to vegetable gardens in a land where the sun's rays burn as hot as embers. Outside the city there is nothing but a desert of sand and rock, held back by a mountain that stretches from one horizon to the other, like an endless rampart. In the midst of this inhospitable desert, life has the aura of a miracle.

Frugality is the norm. Very few people live in extreme poverty in this culture of hospitality and charity, major precepts of Islam that have been perpetuated here forever. The seasons and constellations govern the time. The presence of the age-old, protective mausoleum dedicated to the city's founder, who throughout his entire life teaching non-violence, has for many years created a climate of spirituality conducive to a calm, harmonious environment.

Yet a peaceful society is not a paradise. Here, as elsewhere, people suffer; the best and the worst live side by side. Neighborly values coexist with dissent and jealousy, while women endure conditions that often harm the spirit and the heart. Yet despite everything, a sense of prevailing temperance maintains peace. A sort of overriding joy compensates for the precarious living situations, displayed at every possible occasion in improvised celebrations. Here, life is experienced in a tangible way. The smallest sip of water, the tiniest bite of food gives genuine flavor to life, against a backdrop of ever-lasting patience. Satisfaction and gratitude come easily once basic needs are taken care of, as if every day lived was already a privilege, a reprieve. Death is a familiar face, but not a tragedy. It is cruel when children are taken, but the conviction that the Creator has removed them from the turpitudes of the world to maintain their innocence eases the sorrow. Death is the steward of a finite existence for which everyone is prepared. It is a fact, unaltered by social status, prestige or wealth. It goes about its business, unpredictably, and returns souls to God when their time has come. Acceptance of one's destiny is conducive to a serene heart, as human will is powerless in the face of fate.

It is within this complex world that every day the blacksmith makes his anvil sing. He himself is a singer, a poet, and makes an offering of his art. Playing his cord instrument while he sings, he spreads joy to a large, jubilant group of people who are often almost in a trance-like state, under a sky that is nearly always glittering with incomparably bright stars. This world of dreams and poetry has its share of torments, but it has existed for many long years. As in other places of the world, people here aim for harmony, without entirely achieving it–perfection is not within their realm.

The end of a traditional world

Slowly, insidiously, everything began to shift within this traditional world. The blacksmith grew sad. He was worried, his mind absorbed and anxious. He no longer returned home at dusk like a hunter at the end of the day, sometimes empty-handed, but most often carrying a basket full of food that he earned entirely from his merit, his talent, and his courage, as well as from divine benevolence, to provide for his family. Work was growing perilously scarce for the blacksmith. The French occupiers had discovered coal and were offering all able-bodied men a paid job. The entire society was in turmoil. The era of savoring time as an eternal value was over, replaced by the heretofore-unknown pace of clocks and watches, with their relentless minutes and seconds. The goal of this new time was to eliminate any "wasted time" and, in this land of peaceful daydreaming, indolence was viewed as laziness. The time had come to be serious, to slave away. Every morning, carrying acetylene torches, men dropped into the dark bowels of the earth to extract a black material containing a fire that had gone out long ago, as if just waiting to awake and change the order of the world. Every night, the men emerged from this strange anthill in which they had been sequestered all day, their faces blackened. It was difficult to recognize them until ablutions had cleared off the dark mask of dust and coal that covered their faces. Dark circles remained under their eyes, the sign of the new brotherhood of miners. Watches appeared on more and more wrists; to get around faster, the number of bicycles skyrocketed; money wormed its way into every level of the community. Traditions gradually began to seem old-fashioned, outdated. It was time to start living in sync with the new culture.

The blacksmith resisted these changes for as long as possible. Yet he had to face reality: he had fewer and fewer customers, and feeding his family was becoming nothing short of a miracle. The only thing left to do was to become an ant, like the others. Given his natural ability, he was given the job of driving a switch engine, hauling a long line of carts filled with the magic material, most of which would be exported to France. The large trains with powerful locomotives carried off the black material like thieves. And that is how progress burst into the traditional way of life.

The child was distraught to see the blacksmith return each evening, completely black, like all the others. It was as if his idol had been desecrated. The workshop had become a silent shell behind a door now closed on timeless memories from an era that had changed so brutally. The anvil no longer sang. Civilization had arrived, with its attributes, complexity, and immense powers of attraction–although he was unable to understand it or even less able to explain it. The blacksmith, poet, and musician was my own father, and the child was, of course, me.

The silence of the anvil

The father's servitude inflicted a strange wound on the child. The entire population felt that something important had happened, insidiously, without really knowing what it was. Paralleling this new situation, whereby work itself had become the purpose of life, was the immoderate behavior inspired by money and the desire to buy new things. As if driven by a final burst of freedom, some of the miners did not return to work after receiving their first paychecks. When they returned after a month or two, their employers, displeased, asked them why they hadn't come back sooner. They answered, innocently enough, that they had not yet spent all their money, so why would they go back to work? Without realizing it, they were raising a question that had been carefully avoided, but which many people now view as crucial. In our current era of great turmoil, an answer must be found that provides an alternate view of the human condition: do we work to live or do we live to work? It's easy to imagine just how quickly the coal company set these undisciplined, innocent laborers straight.

    I think I understood much later that this arrogant and totalitarian modern age had somehow obliterated the blacksmith by negating his identity and his individuality—as it had done to countless other people in the North and South. Even worse: under the pretense of improving their living conditions, it had instead reduced everyone to a form of modern-day slavery, not only by producing financial capital without any concern for fairness, but by instituting the worst inequality on the planet, taking money as the only measure of wealth. The exploitation and enslavement of man by man and of woman by man has always been a perversion, a sort of fatality that has tainted human history with an all-to-familiar affliction. But as opposed to what could be called an innate perversion, our contemporary age, which has fostered revolutions supposed to end this exploitation, has perpetuated it under the banner of the loftiest moral declarations: democracy, liberty, equality, fraternity, human rights, the abolition of privileges. The intention may have been sincere, but unfortunately the most tenacious attempts to establish an equitable order have clearly been defeated by the underlying nature of humankind.

The sound of the anvil was never louder for me than when it fell silent, an irrevocable stillness that seemed to have been written on an unfinished score, forever silencing the melody. Later, I came to understand that this silence planted the seeds of a rebellion that finally began to sprout in the late 1950s. I was twenty years old at the time, and I felt that our contemporary age was an immense sham.

2. Disillusionment

In the late 1950s, I was working as a skilled laborer for a company based in the Paris region. My colleagues, whom I liked and respected, were convinced that the modern world held a radiant future for their children; this gave meaning to their drudgery. Adamantly attached to this belief, some of them were as keen as missionaries—even though the ambience was essentially one of atheism and a widely prevailing secularism. They drew on the pervasive ideas of Marxist doctrine as an antidote to any spiritual leanings; they had a highly contentious reaction to any form of religious belief and condemned the "betrayal" of the Church, which they believed was far more closely allied with capital than with the proletariat. Their faith lay in progress, a progress they nearly worshiped, even to the point of self-sacrifice. They said: "We put up with a lot, but it's so that our children will have a better life. They will have the education we didn't get; they will be far from factories; they'll have clean, smooth hands. This will make up for our calloused hands and our servitude." The regret of being uneducated made them feel as if they, along with traditional French farmers, the *paysans*, were among the lowest caste—as is the case in every society that promotes an elite hierarchy based on intellect.

This was the era of postwar France, the "Trente Glorieuses,"[1] which lasted through the mid-1970s, with its many illusions: the economic machine was running full bore, fueled by abundant and nearly free resources from the developing countries. Yet a cloud of disenchantment hung over this society that was supposedly basking in happiness, probably due to overabundance. "France is bored," sometimes appeared as a newspaper headline. In contrast to today, the younger generation could expect to have a glowing future, yet there was a disturbing malaise, as if the excesses of "having" eliminated the needs of "being"—with the consumer society simultaneously creating both needs and frustrations. Consumers were clearly cogs in a machine that was constantly producing more and more, just so that we could continue to consume. Controlling the mind-numbing prod of ubiquitous advertising, it toyed with consumers, like a courtesan using her deceptive charms, promising ever-more euphoric pleasures.

The rebellions of May '68 against the consumer society broke out suddenly within this insidious situation. Among the multiple and complex reasons for this uprising, we can identify one that relates to this discussion—a desire, expressed or latent, for restraint. Excess and happiness do not necessarily go hand in hand; they can even be antithetical. Over and beyond the manifold and largely obsolete causes of the time, this younger generation probably felt that their own creativity would be confiscated by a society that was materially too safe, and locked into a seemingly irreversible path. This echoed my own sentiments, ten years earlier, against the precepts, dogmas, credos of the reigning ideologies, but which were met with indifference and even mistrust at the time. These young people probably

---

1. The "Trente Glorieuses," or "Glorious Thirty," refers to the three decades from 1945 to 1975, a period of economic prosperity and high productivity in France.

yearned for a fate in which risk and the unknown made life more meaningful and appealing. Life is a beautiful adventure only when there are large and small challenges to face; they keep people alert, inspire creativity, stimulate the imagination, and in short, generate enthusiasm–in other words, all that is divine within us. A joie de vivre is a supreme value to which we all aspire, but which cannot be bought, even for billions of dollars. It is a kind of privilege, a gift from a mysterious prince who can grant it to the humblest abode, while withholding it from the most lavish palace.

Quite simply, how can one not take issue with a civilization that has made of a man's tie the symbolic noose of daily strangulation? Is this adornment actually a leash held by the famous invisible hand of the market, imparting a sense of freedom only when it is removed at the end of a laborious day? Semantics often reveal hidden truths: what to make of such expressions as human materials, downsizing, human resources? All these observations actually reveal a fundamental truth, namely, the ridiculously low value of the individual trapped in a society of money and finance–once he or she has fully integrated the system of values based on excellence and competitiveness that starts with early childhood education and promotes all the vanities linked to social success. Yet none of this guarantees an active and fulfilled life.

This indictment is not aimed at individuals, but at the doctrine itself. The modern era inflicted on us has been stripped of the multiple values it claims to support, as if to better betray them. The state of the world, of nature, and of humankind itself reflects this fallacy.

3. Decline of rural life

Since the dawn of time, people have praised Mother Earth and composed poems in her honor. Playing instruments indigenous to their diverse cultures, they have sung the praises of their land and paid homage to its hospitality, its beauty, along with its severity and austerity.

During my childhood in the Sahara, I often saw people preparing for journeys. After kneeling down, they took a handful of earth or sand from their place of birth and that of their ancestors and packed it into a leather pouch. This pouch, tied to their belts, immediately became a talisman that would accompany them on their journeys, helping them feel connected to their homeland wherever they went. The actual place in which lives unfold can transcend mere geography, provided it is imbued with humanity. Insofar as time remains something cosmic, and space is sacred, the individual remains profoundly linked to real life, creating a reality that is in sync with the needs of everyday life.

On this note, I remember an anecdote from a book by Nikos Kazantzakis describing people on Crete fleeing the violence of the Turks. During the sad exodus as they sought refuge, an old man was walking, buckled under the weight of a sack. Some good souls offered to help, but he stubbornly refused. They finally learned that the precious sack contained the bones of the old man's ancestors. Forced to flee without knowing if he could ever return, he took the time to unearth these relics so that he could reseed the land that welcomed him. After breaking the original link with his ancestors, his goal was to reconnect with them and ultimately ease the tragedy of exile. Belonging to a land is absolutely vital for all people. This is what I tried to communicate, with difficulty, to an American aid volunteer working in the Sahel. He lamented the fact that the women had to walk two kilometers to draw water for the village. Unaware of the relationship to the ancestors, he suggested, logically enough, constructing a new village near the water.

The tragedy of exile

Our contemporary age has invented all sorts of exiles. The never-ending war in the trenches from 1914 to 1918 was one of them. I am still appalled and outraged when I think about the plight of the stewards of the land. The mutual genocide of the French and German farmers, for reasons far more perverse than merely defending the homeland, was the apotheosis of cruelty. It was an opportunity to test the most atrocious technological inventions ever created for destruction and death. There is not a single village in France or Germany that did not pay a tribute in blood to this poorly defined cause–or rather one that was too well defined to be credible. Not to mention the countless innocents from colonial territories whose blood irrigated the scarred land of Europe. Some soldiers, even European ones, who could not bear the uprooting and the exile, were apparently so homesick for the villages of their birth that they died of it. There is nothing more poignant than the letters sent by soldiers on the front or in the trenches to their families, to their loved ones at home. These missives, inspired by horror, distilled the most basic aspects of the human condition: physical and psychic suffering, despair, hope, fear of death, etc. Modern civilization, assumed to be a civilizing force for humanity, offers a striking example of barbarity when driven into a corner.

These atrocities are now considered a normal state of affairs and are even glorified during commemorations and ceremonies of remembrance–but without the memories: people have an appetite for archaic rituals, even among societies that rely on reason to claim superiority over these rites. It takes a special kind of hypocrisy not to recognize that this carnage is motivated by anything other than the interests of dark forces whose mission on earth is to inspire the human spirit to mass murder. This aberration not only still prevails, but has spread to the extent that we can no longer examine it from the vantage point of reason alone. It is nearly metaphysical, deeply rooted in the mind and spirit of the human species. Haven't we all heard the incalculably cynical statement that there's nothing like "a good war" to jumpstart the economy?

Industry's need for labor also sparked the massive migration of rural populations to industrial centers, triggering the dismantling of the centuries-old traditional social structures in Europe. The Industrial Revolution owes its success to the physical energy of the *paysan*. As opposed to a mobilization on the battlefield, it offered what appeared to be a positive outcome: escape from the arduous and unpredictable conditions of working the land, and the material comfort and security of a regular salary. "Voluntary servitude" was perceived as a liberation, supported tooth and nail by propaganda that extolled progress. After repeated efforts were made to resolve the quasi-permanent disputes between the capitalist powers and the workforce, the Industrial Revolution managed to convince virtually everyone of its relevance and its benefits, while successfully pillaging the planet. At the same time, it glossed over the basic tenets on which these benefits were built.

A growing number of people in so-called prosperous nations are currently disenchanted and disillusioned. This long process of alienation has now produced a twofold exile: individuals are no longer linked to a genuine social body, nor connected to a territory. Mobility has become the prerequisite for keeping a job. Vibrant culture has been replaced by an encyclopedic mass of knowledge and an amount of information worthy of a television game show. None of this fosters anything other than abstract thought, nor does it create an original and sustaining cultural identity. Everything is increasingly temporary and ephemeral, part of a frenzied movement that is growing exponentially, transforming people into hyperactive productive electrons, suffering from stress-induced illnesses.

Alienation of rural life

The rural world has not escaped the illusions and harm of the modern age. When we returned to the land in 1961, my initially naïve outlook took a beating with this realization. I thought that by turning my back on the urban world I was going to distance myself from an obsession with productivity. Unfortunately, I soon learned that it was equally fierce in the countryside. The indoctrination had been so strong that my young colleagues in the rural family house where I, already the head of a household, was trying to learn the fundamentals of agriculture, were in a nearly irrepressible trance. Virtually every conversation concerned what they had been taught: the miracles of agrochemicals, the miraculous yields they could wrest from the soil. They compared the results of one fertilizer or another, of this or that pesticide applied to a certain pest or invasive fungi. They sounded like warriors. The companies producing so-called plant-protection substances set the tone: product packaging with labels featuring a skull-and-crossbones logo promoted a belligerent approach to living organisms. But the overarching god that determined everything, that received the utmost praise, was the tractor. A symbol of power, a fantasy, and the emblem of technical progress, this machine with all its horsepower would abolish the actual horse, from a bygone age, so that these young people, descendants in a long line of barefooted farm laborers, could join the modern age. They felt this need even more strongly in that the French *paysan* had long been considered mentally unfit for progress. They themselves had even internalized the negative image of the serf, trudging through the fields.

After this first immersion, which was like a rite of passage, my family settled into rural life. All around us was this frenzy to achieve ever-greater crop yields, encouraged by the joint agricultural policy established throughout Europe. This approach was fully justified in a postwar situation, while the country was repairing the destruction it suffered, concurrent with a period of enormous food shortages. It was all hands on deck: production subsidies were allocated to boost a zeal for work; mixed crop and livestock farming were replaced by monoculture farms; bank loans for all sorts of equipment were granted easily, at highly favorable rates; production increased as plots were regrouped and expanded; machinery became increasingly powerful; and fertilizers and pesticides were used on a massive scale, as was specialized seed selection.

I won't pursue these issues, which I have already discussed at great length in other books. The agricultural age in the West came to an end with the disappearance of the small farmers as the age-old stewards of Mother Earth. They participated unwittingly in this unfettered growth and reign of immoderation–whose virulence we now so deplore. The most tragic aspect is that these stewards, manipulated and conditioned by the ideology of the omnipotent profit motive, have destroyed and are continuing to destroy the collective and vital resource that has been their mission to maintain and transmit for posterity. This requires prudent and responsible management, but as we know, the question of preserving this heritage had been excluded from all transactions.

Furthermore, international competition and the law of the marketplace contributed to mutual economic self-destruction, even among the poorest of the small farmers. World hunger, which the modern production system should have eradicated, has instead been compounded by a greed-inspired system. Let us hope that the small farmers who have survived physical and economic destruction understand that they must, for their own salvation, adopt human-scale, diversified farming structures as bastions against the soulless, multitentacled monster of profit. A connection with the earth based on restraint and respect is not only essential to their survival, but also to their dignity. I often dream about the advent of a new farmer, running his small farm as the undisputed sovereign of his own small realm. Given the current economic situation, the financial crisis will certainly bring to light our true wealth, and should logically prompt world governance to challenge the entire model of society. After the profit motive took everything it possibly could, producing shameful wealth from the backs of the farmers, it is now starving them–pending their future elimination altogether.

2

THE SHAM OF THE MODERN AGE

The modern or contemporary age will often be discussed here, not to sing its praises yet again, but as the object of intense criticism. My entirely personal indictment will only become more severe as the extent of the harmful impact of what is probably the most hypocritical ideology in the history of mankind becomes clear. The reasons for the rebellion triggered by the silence of the anvil have multiplied and become even more compelling as the founding myths and goals of the contemporary world have been analyzed and deciphered, revealing its specific nature, as compared to the world of the past. Yet it would be unfair and absurd to deny some of the progress made in politics, technology, and medicine, for example. But instead of adding to earlier achievements, the positive benefits have wiped the slate clean, as if humanity's spirit up to now had been nothing but obscurantism, ignorance, and superstition. We owe the homogeneity and standardization of our entire world, from pole to pole, to this totalitarian arrogance.

1. Progress: between myth and reality

The technology and multiple innovations that fascinate people–promoted as progress for all, but which has turned out to be nothing more than a myth–are only avatars of a quasi-metaphysical principle of nature. Behind the alluring appearances of an era that is supposed to free the human species, we discover an ideology based on the celebration of a self-proclaimed Western demiurge, a being that places itself on the same pedestal as the gods of Olympus through the sheer force of reason, an attribute exalted by the ancient Greeks. This premise, supported by categorical materialistic theories, has whittled what we called spirituality down to a bare minimum–and even, with the full force of materialism, eliminated it from contemporary thought. As a result of the metaphysical assumptions establishing mankind as gods, nature was declared subordinate, while the principle of a planet as a mere source of raw materials to be exploited became the norm. An enlightened mind examining the disastrous impact of this norm on the very foundations of life itself could legitimately wonder whether nature had not brought mankind into being for the sole purpose of being destroyed by it. The hypothesis is absurd. Yet the fact remains: the demiurge, adopting the role of prince of creation, has unleashed predatory impulses that threaten the entire planet itself.

However, so as to not place the entire blame on the modern age, we must remember that the butchering and plundering of our planet and its vital forests occurred as so-called primitive civilizations evolved into more sophisticated ones.[1] The fundamentalism of pure reason, detached from the innate natural intelligence within each and every one of us, has built and structured a parallel world that is now on the verge of collapse.

This choice has also created a universal trap in which our world has fallen, with no means of escape. In the microcosms of our daily

1. See Fairfield Osborn, *Our Plundered Planet* (Boston: Little, Brown and Co., 1948).

lives, we all experience the ever-increasing restrictions and dependencies dictated by modern life. For the last two or three centuries, the modern world has denied and eradicated everything that does not comply with the "inorganic-inspired" way of thinking it established. I take "inorganic thought" to mean the principles produced by radical positivism, which excludes all references to subjectivity, sensitivity, and intuition. Reality is perceived in a fragmented and mechanistic way, supported by a proliferation of specialists–the opposite of the shared and interdependent vision represented by ecology. Like any belief, by definition based on a conviction taken as absolute truth, this approach, characterized by relentless proselytizing, has tried to elevate rationality into a universal value, the only one able to "accurately" comprehend reality. It therefore focuses–not entirely successfully–on stripping people of the convictions and experiences they have acquired subjectively, which pure scientism views as superstition and obscurantism.

But the overarching offence of this regressive approach is to have surrendered beauty, the majesty of life and of individuals themselves to the vulgarity and international order of finance. What we call the financial crisis is just one of its effects: how not to be overcome by anger at seeing life so desecrated by ignorance? Our current world was built on the foundations of a soulless rationality. It has lost its magic and is now fostering disappointment and boredom. An increasing urbanization seems to limit the scope of tangible creativity, while breeding a proliferation of untested concepts, abstract ideas that often prove to be fanciful. Meanwhile, a yearning for more meaning, and a happier and more relaxed life has been rapidly gaining ground. Without undue optimism, but based on a simple observation of facts, it appears that a new approach brought about by the failure of Prometheus is germinating, as the reality of the increasingly dramatic social and ecological situation hits home.

I worked in a factory for three years, alongside French men and women from all over the country and alongside immigrants. In this struggling microcosm, the alienation of individuals with boring, even harmful jobs, was astonishing. The only antidote to this situation? A world with compassion for others, where hearts and fraternity can flourish. And speaking of alienation, is there any need to repeat that the assembly line work glorified by Mr. Taylor had made the individual a biological cog, reduced to nearly mindlessness by repetitive movement? Is there any need to describe the conditions of miners suffering from silicosis, as they extracted minerals and fuels from deep underground to fire blast furnaces? The list goes on. How, then, to reconcile this widespread servitude with humanist declarations? As I myself worked in a warehouse, I had ample experience in this hard-working world of the constraints, and the impact they had on the men working there. If I try to recall it today, the image of a pyramid comes to mind. A hierarchical, quasi-military pyramid with the most important people at the top, wreathed in all the positive aspects–good salaries, respect, authority–and the ensuing benefits; and, at the bottom of the pyramid, individuals surrounded by all the negative ones: low pay and mediocre living conditions. Between the two are the various rungs to climb and pitfalls to avoid. These are the steps to development and excellence, as laid out by the educational system in force. I remember, in particular, a clearly substandard painting workshop, where the poor workers risked their health and entire well-being, after contributing their skills and their labor, merely for the chance of surviving on a meager wage. In this human beehive, work was glorified as a great virtue, fueling an ever-expanding productivity. Such a scenario has been central to the intangible tenet of unlimited economic growth, as any transgression or challenge to this principle has until now been seen as a schism; in an earlier age, it could have meant being burned at the stake.

 Looking objectively at the conditions imposed on people on the pretext of progress that was promoted wholeheartedly as liberating, I could never fend off the feeling that the system was nearly prison-like. I often discuss this issue during my conferences, drawing the public's attention to the lives of individuals within this context: they are imprisoned from preschool to university. The vocabulary we now use is eloquent: we are in a daily grind, a nine-to-five rat race, on a treadmill, in a rut. Whether people realize it or not, everything is narrow and small in the life of a city-dweller, starting with the lack of a horizon. The job of television, with its images reflecting a vast world beyond, is to make us temporarily forget this fact. This quasi-penal world has reached its peak with the proliferation of keys, locks, door codes, surveillance cameras, and so on. An environment of such suspicion and protection can obviously only produce social toxins that exacerbate feelings of insecurity by creating actual barriers, both inside and out.

But there exists an insidious and pernicious bondage that is even more disturbing: the exponential use of electronic and computing devices that directly affect the human psyche. They seem to be effectively molding new generations with remarkable efficiency. The handwritten word, an age-old means of communication, is being replaced by the screen. Could it, however, be of some use for breaking down the solitude of a society in increasing need of social connections, whether they be face-to-face or not? Perhaps the modern age is actually winning, slowly but surely, the battle for the definitive alienation of individuals, by rendering them dependent on tools purporting the liberate them. This seems to be a way of cloning and standardizing minds on a global scale–as anyone who travels can attest. Our prior experiences nourish our imaginations. Our brains could not have evolved without a link to a collective brain; yet in our current computing nebula, they may have been reduced to a sort of biological electronic component, receiving and transmitting data, without any clear awareness of the impact for the overall evolution of the human species. Thinking that the human brain can emerge unscathed from the transfer of its extraordinarily complex and subtle functions to sophisticated machines is highly unrealistic—especially without any understanding of its impact on the overall evolution of the human species. By creating these tools, has the brain made itself obsolete? This issue is more serious than most people think. Even a less complex tool like a car incorporates the driver as a biological component in the complexity of elements that ensure its movement. The feeling of freedom and power felt by the driver is derived from a vehicle that adheres to mechanical principles, a fact that becomes obvious with the slightest breakdown or empty gas tank.

Restraint should perhaps also be used against the current trend suggesting that access to every piece of information, everywhere and anytime, is actually a sign of freedom. Information presented as an absolutely indisputable truth can actually be the worst kind of misinformation. Given that any hoax or sham is possible, there is some cause to worry about the future of the "truth," which is one of the pillars of an enlightened society. We are now seeing the emergence of a hypermarket of information, where anything and everything is available; everyone can issue lies and denials. Many publications are merely compilations of data drawn from an immense pool of facts and events, interpreted to support any individual argument. In the complex sea of virtue and villainy, it will become increasingly difficult for the honest citizen to form an opinion. Lost in a maze of "for" and "against," of "pro" and "con," and after shouting—"What's the outcome?"—"Where is the truth?"—"What is the truth?"—people can always opt the soothing energy of silence, beautiful silence. How wonderful! Embarking on an information fast from time to time, as a purification, is probably one of the most beneficial acts of restraint.

This raises a dilemma. A new power seems to have emerged from this ambiguous nebula: that of legalized indiscretion, which worms itself into the most intimate and confidential corners of our existence. Has the time come to extricate ourselves from a morbid, nearly spellbound fascination, in order to admire what life has to offer and reconnect with sensitivity and intuition so as to grasp the tangible message of reality? Our integrity cannot be breeched by any mere tool if we remain conscious and aware. Moderation is one of the ways in which the human spirit can truly serve the individual and natural life. No other age in history has created so many levels of dependency as our modern era. The only purpose of so many tools seems to have to make the overall frenzy bearable, whereas it is essential to challenge this situation as the major anomaly it is. It is perhaps time to gradually reintroduce an existence where rhythm and tempo, tools and methods, are controlled by an individual and collective awareness that is finally free of illusion. And in that, restraint has a role to play.

2. Domination of the profit motive

The initial principle and original intent of the modern age, drawing on the achievements of the Industrial Revolution, could have provided an opportunity for humanity. But a fatal mistake occurred, and we are only now starting to understand its disastrous impact with the current crisis: the entire collective fate, beauty, and nobility of planet earth was made subservient to the iniquity of finance. And with this, the die was cast. Anything that did not have a price did not have any value. Money, an invention intended to standardize bartering and exchange, a noble medium used to represent effort, imagination, creativity, and the useful products of life, was denatured by the concept of capital that accrues while you sleep. These reflections are trite today, yet the impact of finance is far more widespread than that discussed in the learned theories of Nobel prizewinners in pseudo-economy. We must remember that what we call "economy" consists of a system that through its dissipating and destructive nature is actually a denial–a genuine contempt for economy.

Once again, we can only note the ability of semantics to deceive minds, to skillfully maintain misconceptions. For an innocent mind, the economy is a magnificent art that exists to manage and regulate exchanges and the division of resources–all this with a minimum of dissipation and for the well-being of all, by avoiding unnecessary, excessive expenses that would harm assets and common property. Greed and waste are antithetical to this system. This principle of economy has been a constant throughout the entire history of human existence. The well-known symbol of the squirrel, the hardworking ant that refuses a loan to the devil-may-care grasshopper, and the bee that gathers what it needs to survive through the winter are all about saving, not speculating. Humans, however, seem to be the only creatures to have introduced dissipation into a reality governed by a principle expressed as "nothing is lost, nothing is created, everything is transformed."

During a TV program, a man who had become extremely rich was asked if he felt like a predator; discussing the struggle of species to survive he claimed that he was merely following the established rules of life. This exchange avoided the essential issue: he needed to be shown once again that human predatory behavior is not the same as what occurs among animals. When a lion eats an antelope, it is satisfied with the offering of life. It doesn't have a bank or warehouse where it stores antelope. There are photographs of lions drinking water alongside a zebra, an antelope, or any other animal which it hunts, because once the lion is sated, all the animals can drink from the same pond–even though some predators do seize on this easy opportunity to catch their prey.

Humans have moved far away from this basic reality, based on survival and perpetuation of the species, and have become trapped by their own fantasies. We place an exorbitant symbolic value on metal and stones, elevated to symbols of wealth for the rich.

Amerindians watched the arrival of frenetic hordes of European conquerors searching for gold, with the ensuing violence and murders, and genuinely believed that this metal made people go crazy. They were careful to avoid touching it, so as not to be infected by the madness it caused. I have often been amazed by the powerful ability of innocence to reveal profound truths. And in fact, gold has made humanity crazy. It's heartbreaking to see the subliminal power of what is, after all, just a metal.

We can therefore question why so much irrational behavior has had such a tragic impact throughout all of history—and whether gleaming stones like diamonds deserve the sacrifice of an entire miner's life, relegated to the bowels of the earth, just so that elegant women can display them under the ostentatious chandeliers of gala receptions to confirm their status among the wealthy caste. Even though none of this protects them from any of life's turmoils. On occasion, when the trappings of appearance have been swept aside, a moral distress can appear among this triumphant caste, a distress that can even inspire compassion.

The list of all the superfluous things throughout history that have plunged society into major upheavals at the expense of the basic needs, would be long indeed. Even such a commonplace contemporary tool as the car, an eminently practical and useful means of transportation, is most often presented as an object of fantasy representing freedom, power, escape, happiness, sex appeal, and so on. Advertising has brilliantly invented subliminal manipulation techniques to encourage people to purchase cars, which while legal, are not all that different from those used by cults. And to further intensify the pleasure of consuming, it advises us to enjoy it all "to our heart's content."

Excessiveness seems to be the offspring of human subjectivity, a quest to escape the banality of everyday life by opening an unlimited field of ever-changing, always unfulfilled, and competing desires. The goal is to inspire the envy of one's peers through appearances.

Being envied is an important aspect in the mimetic process set in motion to stimulate desire. But there are sometimes inaccessible desires, unattainable because they are too expensive to achieve. Yet this frustrating situation can also be a powerful stimulus for acquisition, which plays into the dynamic of excessive behavior. Comparison and mimetism then become causes of suffering, while a spirit of restraint can overcome desire, creating a profound sense of well-being within us–something the object of our desires cannot provide us.

Traditional cultures, governed by a natural and spontaneous sense of restraint (whereby "we belong to the earth"), are being replaced by excessive civilizations ("the earth belongs to us") that are the vectors of their own eradication. This historic–and recent–phenomenon draws on the accomplishments of technological efficiency to exacerbate and accelerate the process of its own finite existence. The paradigm of energy combustion has created a new order on the entire planet; the perception of time and space has been profoundly altered. Technology has granted its inventors and those who benefit from it a power unrivaled since the dawn of time, but because our consciousness has not evolved sufficiently to master and use these innovations for constructive purposes, the risk of serious abuse remains a clear and present danger.

Man as demiurge is thrilled by the power of pure reason, through which he can transgress rules and natural limitations that have existed since the dawn of time. While early man sought harmony with nature, Promethean man has worked to subordinate, dominate, and exploit it as he pleases. The legend of King Midas who transformed everything he touched into gold is an apt illustration of the spirit of our times. The lesson, of course, is that gold is inedible.

We have thus shifted from an agrarian and pastoral civilization to the glorification of inorganic material, triggering widespread damage to the biosphere, as has now become dramatically clear. Moving from real horsepower to steam horsepower considerably increased the influence of the West over other cultures. finally, sophisticated military equipment has led to unprecedented hegemony, notably with the confiscation and annexation of land from legitimate occupants.

Europe's quest to conquer also set up a world order that created the infamous gulf between the northern and southern hemispheres by establishing the absolute and overarching god that we call "finance," with the ensuing disparities. The citizen who has no salary and no resources loses his or her social identity, becoming merely a statistic factored into the minimum level of national prosperity. This "function" is so well integrated and commonplace in the social scheme that it does not even generate any indignation anymore. The citizen's existence–one that can hardly be considered a life–is now owed to social assistance provided by the government, charity organizations, or civil society. Meanwhile, wealthy citizens, viewing this suffering empty shell of a human, get the pleasant feeling that they somehow have good karma. This fragmented, partitioned, and restructured society that creates ever-greater anxiety simultaneously promulgates anti-anxiety medication so as to withstand an everyday reality that the heart and mind can only, in all logic, disavow.

Individuals afflicted with a sort of "lucrepathy" (a pathological love of money) are above all driven by a founding myth. They are possessed by what they believe they possess. Economists, with their figures, formulas, and ratios, can explain the mechanisms of a seemingly rational phenomenon, but they overlook the most important parameter: finance is essentially a nearly metaphysical belief, firmly rooted in human subjectivity. From this unassailable position, finance becomes an all-consuming obsession, a patron deity, playing at will with hope and despair, and dominating countries. It creates a self-centered feeling of power that is probably an antidote to the fear of insignificance and of the finite existence of human life–a human life that seems ridiculous when it is separated from the beauty, the luxuriance, of the world. Otherwise, how else to understand this phenomenon's grip over reality? Money that was originally hard coin has been transformed into a fluid, a spirit that blows where it pleases, exacerbating frustrations with the sole aim of perpetuating its absolute authority. We manufacture weapons that are a disgrace to our species and have set up an anthropophagic order known as globalization, all for the benefit of "finance."

3. Breakdown of universal principles

The importance of time and money in contemporary society has broken down the millennia-old rhythms by which the human race has been organized. Time does not, in fact, exist without our sense and perception of it. It is a sort of illusion that gives a comprehensible framework to our lives; without it, there would be only eternity, a world without time.

The modern world has profoundly modified the eternal, universal parameters that provided anthropology with a referential grid which could be applied to the entire human species prior to the Industrial Revolution. Every ethnic group was part of an earthly, cosmic, and temporal reality. What differed from one group to another was the perception of this reality–along with questions concerning life, death, love, suffering–indeed, everything relating to metaphysics. Anthropology has made considerable progress in deciphering the human phenomenon, but much more needs to be done. We only have to attempt some self-reflection to see just how difficult it is to know oneself. These issues must be approached with humility, with the aim of contributing, as much possible, to the higher goal of humanization, without which our existence on earth has no meaning.

In nearly all traditional societies, time did not seem to have any particular structure. It was as if immobile, an entity on which humans recorded their cycles: births, deaths, relationships. After the "nontime" of primitive cultures, agrarian civilization probably acquired a more tangible perception of time, with periods of rest and work determined, at least in our regions, by the seasons. This kind of time is cosmic in scope. For the earliest humans, who cared nothing for birthdays or other such milestones, time probably did not pass, but rather they themselves moved toward some kind of elsewhere, one that was as real as life on earth. In our era, time definitely goes by, especially as it is now indexed to money. As a result, we must never lose time, but always save it and spend it–a principle that has established frenetic movement as a collective mode of existence. It is fragmented into hours, minutes, and seconds by a vigilant array of clocks, watches, and chronometers. The god Chronos himself would be disconcerted by a hysteria that even he could never have imagined. In track-and-field events, a fraction of a second makes the difference between victory and defeat; the faces of athletes contorted by the extreme effort demanded of their poor bodies illustrate the obsessional nature that is the rule of the game. This abnormal frenzy, a collective pathology that we either do not want to or cannot give up, has inspired the invention of tools for high-speed communication and travel. The rhythms are frenetic; the lack of time, constant. It is a machine that harasses everyone, creating an insidious and paralyzing sense of anxiety, causing pain and stiffness in bodies that are constantly mistreated by day-to-day desires: from the top to the bottom of the social hierarchy, everyone must spend their lives being productive. The ratio of waste produced by such as system illustrates the irrationality of what is supposed to be rational behavior.

Furthermore, with computers, the notion of time has now taken an unpredictable but decisive turn. They allow us to instantly access any bit of information in the world, to communicate with people across vast distances. They are among the magical tools that have reduced time and space to such a degree that these have very nearly been abolished. A temporal bubble has formed between the concept of time based on eternal cosmic cycles and that of a hysterical, uprooted civilization. Paradoxically, it imposes a psychological sense of time experienced as infinitely compressible or expandable, unhindered by the usual models. It throws us off balance. And yet our heartbeats, the rhythm of our breathing, and the blood circulating in our veins constantly remind us that we are connected to a cosmic clock, rather than to the pistons of our combustion engines.

Ultimately, when the tools designed to save time are used for ever-more efficient and unlimited productivity, they lose their purpose. "Westerners invent tools to save time and are then forced to work day and night," my third-world friends used to tell me.

It's a valid question as to whether virtual time, which is increasingly becoming the matrix defining the existence of modern mankind, might not adversely affect the profound nature of the individual, given just how out of kilter it makes us feel. I once asked some friends if their son, a student, lived with them. They said that he did, but without really being there. I finally understood that he physically lived in the same house, but that his mind was entirely caught up in his keyboard, mouse, and screen, and that he was, in fact, someplace far away. He was captivated, nearly bewitched, by these prodigious tools. He had joined a new type of brotherhood of ghosts, with whom he carried on a dialogue that he could no longer maintain with his family. But because virtual meals have not yet been invented, his one concession to his family was a fleeting appearance at the dinner table.

Mistaking communication for relationship can seriously interfere with the quest to achieve real time, a genuine, shared moment, something that increasing numbers of people yearn for as a vital necessity. Authentic social bonds in our lives cannot be broken without causing serious harm. Communication tools, remote controls, and computers will always have large storage capacities, but never genuine memories. Do they strengthen social bonds or do they instead merely connect poles of solitude? The Internet has the undeniable benefit of freeing information from the arbitrary censorship of the powers that be. As such, it contributes to planetary awareness. But it is also the antithesis of this, as it can convey, propagate, and share all the world's wickedness. Like all the tools invented by mankind, it can be used for the best and worst purposes, depending on the evolution and awareness of the individual using it.

It is disturbing to note that sophisticated tools often require people to adapt their ways of life to the functional requirements of these tools. With their ever-expanding range of influence, our technological innovations may just take away our ability to act with simple, manageable, and sustainable methods. The complex instruments that are supposed to serve the human community are actually in the process of enslaving it. Ivan Illich demonstrated this with what he calls the "backlash of tools." The complexity of their mechanisms are beyond the scope of the user and require increasingly specialized personnel to repair them. Who today knows how to fix a computer, a cell phone, or a television? And cars, which used to have fairly simple parts that owners could fix themselves, have become off-limits to even experienced amateur mechanics.

The modern world, now based on tools that are entirely dependent on conventional energy, is clearly, and despite appearances, the most vulnerable era that has ever existed. The idea of exhausting the sources of electrical energy and fossil fuels—a situation that would paralyze the entire system, rendering it obsolete overnight—is inconceivable. Were this to happen, it is the communities without all this sophisticated technology that will escape disaster. These communities depend essentially on metabolic energy—the human body, animal traction—and on the elements, all techniques promoted by modern ecological practices. Furthermore, as human perversion is seemingly boundless, we also know that scrambling and destroying the communication equipment of the "enemy" is a priority of strategic military research. It's easy to imagine the vulnerability of a nation doomed with deafness as well as blindness, when all its screens go blank.

Some would say this is pure science fiction, overlooking the fact that many theories once viewed as completely convoluted in their times have been proven true over time. Most of the current phenomena caused by human behavior, and its disastrous impacts, were once held to be impossible. Aldous Huxley's *Brave New World*, for example, was seen as a farfetched, unrealistic tale when it was published. Today, we now know that the reality is even worse. Such a denial is probably due to the fact that modern prophecies, based on objective criteria alone, formulate projections and forecasts according to a strictly rational model. They do not take into account one essential factor: human subjectivity. A stock market crash is not merely caused by a dysfunctional financial system; it can also be widely attributed to such subjective parameters as fear, greed, ambition, and so on.

It will always be impossible to understand how the world works without factoring in human irrationality. The worst violence, including war, is caused by beliefs, nationalism, ideology, myths, and symbols, far more than by the overt reasons often invoked, such as territory, which are merely alibis. One among many examples: the Israeli–Palestinian conflict, which has provoked so much suffering and destruction, cannot be explained by a simple question of space. Symbolic and religious issues have severely handicapped any resolution. Technology, with all its accomplishments and miracles, has not yet invented a machine to measure egotism, greed, ambition, fears, virtues, and flaws. These tools could incorporate the most decisive data impacting societal development. To reiterate: positive change in the world will only come about through positive change in individuals. There is no other way.

The context today is confusing, and it is increasingly difficult to know who is responsible for the serious harm done to life everywhere. It is as if the complexity of the system had absorbed the human conscience, abilities, and impulses as the basic components of an order that restricts and even abolishes the major attribute of the individual–that of free will. Even those who reject the established order are condemned to support it with their everyday actions: purchasing goods and lighting homes; using water, telephones, computers, and cell phones; and transportation. I have often regretted my inability to avoid the contradiction of polluting the atmosphere with my car and the airplanes I take to promote ecology and agroecology. Our deepest aspirations and our behaviors are rarely completely in sync, and we have to deal with reality. Yet it is crucial to work toward a greater integration, so that this incoherence is no longer viewed as the norm, and even less as inevitable. We should grasp any opportunity we can to pursue a coherent path–and above all, never minimize the importance and power of small resolutions, which are anything but insignificant; indeed, they contribute to a world to which more and more of us now aspire. At least that's how I feel.

3

RESTRAINT, AN ANCESTRAL WISDOM

It has always been difficult for me to define and describe the concept of "restraint" that I have been pursuing for so many years. Choosing it as a way of life is already a major decision, but it involves so much more. It can be viewed as a deliberate stance, a protest against a society of overconsumption; in this case, it is a form of resistance against extreme consumerism. It can be justified by a belief in fairness, in a world where overabundance exists alongside poverty. Religions have made this approach a virtue, an ascetic lifestyle. In reality, it's all this, but there's more. I haven't found any better way to express it than with the following story.

1. An African village

There is an African village in the middle of a semi-arid region the Arabs call the "Sahel," a region threatened by desertification. Figuratively speaking, "Sahel" means "the shore" of the immense ocean of sand that is the Sahara Desert. In reality, this area, between the large desert to the north and the tropical forest to the south, is slowly dying in the wake of the devastating drought of the 1970s that decimated the flora, fauna, livestock, and soil. People are subsisting in precarious conditions, more or less, and the situation can be dire. Yet the life force, omnipresent despite everything, remains stubbornly alive, persisting in the spindly vegetation and the scrawny animals searching for a meager meal. It prevails in the hearts of these miraculously joyful and hard-working women, and these men, who are seemingly powerless prisoners of an age-old indolence. From time to time, small gusts of warm wind appear out of nowhere, whipping up dancing whirlwinds of dust, skimming over the land and then disappearing without a trace. Dried stalks of millet, corn, and sorghum stand in the fields, their grains removed. The harvest has just ended.

The young farmers are jubilant, filling the square, surrounding the village elder who is crouching on a mat, wearing simple clothes, leaning against the ocher dirt wall of his home. He's handsome–not that he has finely chiseled features, but because his worn face and white beard express the extraordinary serenity of the blind: he lives in a profound world of silence and dreams. He seems turned in on himself. He is nobility incarnate, from time to time waving a fan in the warm, drowsy air, where time seems to have stopped outright. The young farmers are respectful, deferring to this man who will soon join the ancestors. After the elder indicates that he's listening, that he had emerged from his private world, one of the young men begins to speak: "Elder, we have come to bring you good news. The harvest was good this year. The land was generous, thanks to the munificence of the heavens, which has sufficiently nurtured and watched over it. We have enough until the next harvest."

The old man expresses his joy with a shout and says: "Let us be grateful to the earth and the sky that nurtured it. I am happy for us all."

After a moment of silence, the young farmers begin to speak again: "We must also tell you that the powder the white men gave us, which we spread over the plot to the east of the village, produced twice the normal harvest. It is more effective than manure and gives us hope for the future."

The old man remains silent for a moment, as if he has returned to his inner sanctum. The young farmers are somewhat taken aback by his lack of enthusiasm. And finally he speaks: "My children, I don't know what this powder contains. But it seems to be a gift from God to have such a beneficial power over the earth, and therefore over our own lives. This will also have another benefit; since it produces such abundant crops, as you say, we can now cultivate just half of our fields, and perhaps even less than that, God willing. We will not have to work so hard. In any case, let us maintain moderation in all things, so that we will always be satisfied in body and soul. And if we have more than we need, let us not forget those who do not, because God provides so that we, too, can give."

This small scene, inspired from a real event, is something of a moral tale. We don't know if the young farmers responded to the elder with enthusiasm or irritation. Maybe they viewed the old man not as a wise elder but as a voice from the past, trapped in a backward vision while they had entered a new era of productivity–a vision that had slowly wormed its way into people's minds. It was an insidious way of preparing the farming communities to join those who had already sworn allegiance to the absolute supremacy of money. The rest is history. These people, who had once been self-sufficient, would be brainwashed into producing exportable goods, to the detriment of their own food security and survival. They would therefore contribute to the "inflow" of currency, on the pretext of modernizing their country. They had to add chemical substances to the soil to achieve higher yields. The problem is that these chemicals are derived from oil, an expensive material they do not produce. Thus they found themselves bound to the laws of the market, thrown into the ring, ruled by the implacable laws of competition, where they would always lose. Destitution then spread, driving increasing emigration.

There's no point belaboring these mechanisms of excess, which generate poverty. These people will be conditioned to become pawns in cynical strategies that propel them from a place of restraint into impoverishment, as described by Majid Rahnema in his book, *Quand la misère chasse la pauvreté* (Actes Sud, 2003). This scheme is so complex that people are powerless to control it, in the absence of a strict ethical code followed by all, for the good of everyone. The earth, our Mother Earth, then becomes a source of money, an approach that is responsible for the destruction of traditional local organizations, as well as for the massive inequalities on the planet.

Not long ago, in an African village of 200 people, it would have been nearly impossible to put together the equivalent of 150 euros. How could these populations survive without money? Quite simply because money did not exist for them, it served no purpose. Their survival did not depend on dollars. Basic necessities were taken care of through exchange and barter, methods worthy of a Nobel Prize in economy. Furthermore, there was no social security, insurance, or retirement. For the latter, children provided for their parents, according to a principle of direct mutual assistance between all generations. Communities were close to the sources of life–or survival: their land, water, seeds, knowledge, and expertise. They built their own homes with the help of the community. They also met their own intangible and cultural needs. They did not merely form a social group resulting from migration patterns, but rather a social body in which individuals had a role and was useful to themselves and to others. The power of the social bond, albeit no guarantee of ideal relationships, was to abolish solitude. Individuals were not identified merely by a physical and moral reality, but as souls, in the fullest sense of the term, as immortal spirits with a highly specific purpose: they would continue to exist as an ancestor. Regardless of what we may think of these beliefs, they provided solace in the face of death, which has become a terrifying concept in our modern world.

To return to this short story: how to interpret the restraint the blind old man was recommending to his community, which lives under the constant threat of shortages? It cannot be understood through simple logic alone. Something subtle–which I observed with my own grandmother–seems to inspires this outlook, which seems baffling from our point of view. What is this feeling, or intuition, that arises from the depths of an age-old wisdom, which creates this beautiful spirit of temperance, expressed by the simple act of saying "That's enough?" And the gratitude that fills our souls, making every moment of our lives richer and more fulfilling, and conferring a singular lightheartedness to our presence on earth– that of calm and rewarding restraint.

2. The year 1985

The year was 1985, in a conference room somewhere near Lyon: a hundred or so people had come together to discuss agroecology. I had been asked to share my experience on the subject and how this method has been used in developing countries, particularly Burkina Faso. I explained that the country is slightly larger than the state of Colorado, with a population at the time of some seven to eight million people, 96 percent of whom were small farmers.

The national budget was the same as that of the Paris Opéra.[1] The average annual income for a small farmer was approximately 50 dollars. As one of the so-called underdeveloped countries, it ranked at the bottom of the global prosperity scale, as represented by its Gross Domestic Product (GDP) and Gross National Product (GNP). A Laotian friend in his fifties was also attending, and I asked him to share his memories about his community when he was a child. He walked up to the board, sketched a simple diagram and said: "Our village had about 250 people living alongside a river in the forest. We grew rice, our staple food. Every family lived in a strongly built home made from the materials at hand, cultivating their own plot of land, whose size depended on how much work the buffalo could do. The harvests ensured enough food for us and was stored in granaries along the village's main path. The river provided each family with fish to augment our diet of grains, fruits, and vegetables. Mutual support, solidarity, and reciprocity was a given; every year, fishing expeditions were organized to amass a stock of dried fish. The community took care of widows, orphans, the elderly, and the disabled. Traditional healers took care of the ill and watched over the health of everyone. Our multifaceted levels of craftsmanship took care of all our needs: clothing, furniture, shoes, and tools. A bhikku settled disputes and was responsible for social harmony. The overall sentiment, inspired from Buddhist practice, was that everything is sacred. When I felt I had to urinate, while standing on a boat in the middle of the river, it was unthinkable to do so without asking forgiveness from the river for the defilement I would inflict upon it. The only cloud on the horizon: the pattern of constantly clearing land for crops, which damaged the integrity of the natural environment." (Needless to say, an agroecology project should put an end to these practices.) And to conclude, my friend added: "One day, an expert commissioned by the World Bank stayed with us to

---

[1]. In 2010, the Paris Opéra's budget was 192 million euros.

study our way of life. After examining all the parameters, he drew up his report. This report for the World Bank concluded that this community, while pleasant, could not develop because it spent too much time on unproductive activities."

The lesson here was that, even though the village ensured all it basic necessities in a harmonious way, it did not create financial wealth. Thus, in the vocabulary of the pseudo-economy: we do not live off the earth, but off dollars; the dollar is the measure of wealth. Fortunately, a large number of traditional communities still manage to cling to true wealth—but for how much longer?

Overfed populations that have devoted body and soul to the power of the golden calf have clearly abandoned this genuine and natural wealth, but how to communicate this argument? These issues place us at the heart of a set of problems that have overturned traditional social structures—structures that are often criticized by "civilizing forces" for annihilating individual freedom, because the laws of the social body must be obeyed. Money, and money alone, now defines the exact measure of wealth, poverty, or destitution.

The expert's report was duly conveyed to the country's political leaders who, having studied in prestigious Western universities and assimilated their precepts, dogmas and credos, were fully imbued with "contemporary" concepts. They viewed the "archaic nature" of their people with concern and even a touch a shame, seeing it as their mission to elevate the level of "true" civilization. A process of modernization was thus launched, perpetuating the sweeping eradication of tradition that had already been achieved in Europe. Colonizing minds goes hand in hand with colonizing territory. We must not forget that the hegemony of modern civilization over existing cultures first played out in Europe, once a multicultural continent. Travelers throughout Europe during the centuries preceding the Industrial Revolution were astonished and enchanted with its diversity of cultures, languages, dialects, habitats, costumes, customs, food, artistic expression, rites, and beliefs. These autonomous people were not necessarily safe from small or large potentates of evil intent, who used their caste to take advantage of labor, or a clergy preaching acceptance of a divine destiny: when democracy and human rights were trampled, the lives of people in Europe were at times miserable. Indeed, revolutions broke out to fight the arbitrary nature of life and the widespread exploitation–upheavals that often put in power a different set of privileged people or even a system of governance based on horrific repression, as has happened so frequently throughout history.

3. Nothing is lost, nothing is created, everything is transformed

What we call the "economy" is actually the negation of economy. Humanity has never before dissipated so much on the pretext of acquiring resources and goods for its survival. The principle of entropy has never been so triumphant. Yet nature itself, provides us with a magnificent example of economy, the underlying principle of its sustainability. Antoine Lavoisier's famous saying, "nothing is lost, nothing is created, everything is transformed," clearly reveals that nature does not throw anything away. Nature abhors waste, even if it also confounds us with its excessive production of pollen and spermatozoids–only a tiny amount of which is needed for fertility. The farmers with whom I lived in the Cévennes offered me one of my first lessons in economy. At first glance they may have seemed tightfisted, but they were actually keenly aware of the value of things, given the effort required to obtain them, and also, it seems to me, because these things were viewed as sacred. They used to say grace around the large family table and, inspired by a sense of gratitude, consecrated the precious food with the sign of the cross on a loaf of bread, before breaking it. A religious practice? Certainly, but not exclusively. I have always felt that this practice is linked to a feeling once shared by the entire human race.

Farmers in the Cévennes region

As a farmhand in the Ardèche, I was fortunate to have been able to share the lives of several small farmers in the Cévennes, with whom I still maintain a strong bond and great affection. How to forget elderly Froment who, despite–or rather because of–his eighty-five years, still kept up his routine. Early to rise, after a frugal breakfast he would take me out to his worksites where I served as his laborer, rebuilding the collapsed walls that held up his terraced vineyards. Although he was slightly deaf and his memory was starting to fail, he was a spiritual father to me; he had no education or precept other than untroubled manual labor, where every gesture reflects a millennia-old ritual in its precision. I have never seen a true *paysan* run, either in the northern or southern hemisphere; if forced, they do so awkwardly.

One day, during the grape harvest, I saw old Froment looking dumbstruck when, as he stooped over to pick up some seeds that had fallen on the ground, his son-in-law, a farm operator, snapped at him, telling him to go faster, that it was a waste of time, unproductive, to gather the seeds. The tractor's rumbling and exhaust fumes as it towed the trailer reminded us that the bucolic era was long gone. Work in the field was soon about to enter into the trance of industrial progress. The earth should no longer produce food, but rather spit out money.

How to forget Monsieur and Madame Dubois and their little farm in the Cévennes, lost up in the hills overlooking a deep valley, where the roar of the mountain stream only amplified the all-encompassing silence? I spent the winter in these slopes, so steep that, as the local expression goes, dogs have to sit down to bark.

Time here felt limitless. The Dubois home seemed to be drilled into the rock. I stayed there to help M. Dubois with his work; in exchange, he taught me how to weave wicker. Everything was simple: we cooked and heated the house with the fireplace, and ate well-balanced, healthy, and copious traditional food. At night, neighbors appeared in the shadows, carrying an extra log under their arms to add to the fire. We all stayed awake, enjoying the roast chestnuts, talking around the flames, sharing news and making useful objects from rye straw. The guests left late into the night, everyone retreating to their freezing cold rooms, where they warmed up their beds and slid into a thick wool mattress under a warm feather quilt; the lightness and opulence created unrivaled comfort for a perfect night's sleep.

This was one of the most beautiful examples illustrating the power of restraint, in the very heart of a nation that, with its Trente Glorieuses, was glorifying consumption as a lifestyle–one that the upheavals of 1968 tried to overturn. I also remember the craftsmen who were still plying their trades in peace and quiet. The Ducros brothers, from the village near our farm, were coopers and cartwrights, experts in age-old traditions. They acquired new machinery; combining tradition and modern techniques, they became carpenters–to save the family honor–and with their extraordinary skill, were able to produce magnificent objects. These small machine shops, and so many others, seemed to form a family brotherhood. With the advent of a new era, large retail stores, heavy industry, centralization, transportation, and technocratic planning–vaunting their extreme efficiency–all contributed to undermining the foundations of a time-honored order of human affairs. A way of life that once had so much talent and so many spheres of creativity was overwhelmed by a monstrous system that consumes and spits us out, without any other purpose than to serve a blind, cruel and idiotic plutocracy. It's easy for some people who support progress to brand these thoughts as antiquated. Yet the increasing number of dead-ends facing the contemporary world will force us to return to a good number of practices from the past. This is why it's urgent to protect everything on our planet that is still on a human scale, before we reach the end of the "petrolithic" age.

Ancestral wisdom

When I pursue this question of restraint more deeply, I feel much the same as the first human beings must have done, with the sense that nothing truly belonged to them. What to say about these people who, despite the pervasive abundance, remained moderate in behavior? The Sioux people, of whom I am particularly fond, only killed what they needed for survival during their major buffalo hunting expeditions–even though these animals were widespread and even overabundant. Nothing in these sacrificed animals was squandered; waste was forbidden by a sacred moral code, as an offense against nature and its underlying principles. Gratitude for the earth's profusion was a given. This restraint in the face of abundance is a true lesson in nobility. I would like to evoke the Chief Seattle's magnificent speech to the American president, who had proposed purchasing the land of his people: "I am a savage and I do not understand any other way. I have seen a thousand rotting buffaloes on the prairies left by the white man who shot them from a passing train."

Basically none of these native people killed unless it was a vital need; hunting for pleasure was simply inconceivable, as this would have been an outright desecration, an outrageous assault on the force of life and the immanent spirit that governs it. Despite everything, mankind has brought forth people who have based their existence on moderation and restraint, through rituals of gratitude and reconciliation ceremonies. While linking them spiritually to the mystery of life, this temperance also gave them strength, legitimacy, and joyfulness. There were obviously exceptions to this rule here and there, but very few.

The list of actions and behaviors demonstrating the restraint, respect, and gratitude of our ancestors is, however, a long one–before the advent of unlimited greed toward the magnificent gifts of life. I can only imagine the sense of freedom these people must have felt. It reminds me of Mohand, a shepherd friend during my childhood who took care of all the goats and sheep in our community, which were brought together in a single herd early in the morning. He wandered along the paths, wearing rough leather sandals, his rod over his shoulders, a song always on his lips–occasionally interrupted by shouts to the bleating animals–as he climbed large dunes of rock and sand. I was so envious I wanted to bolt, to join the procession which for a second stood out against the blue sky before disappearing behind a mountain, leaving me to my dissatisfaction. I was to supposed to think about getting to school; learn to read, write, and count; become knowledgeable–a refrain I heard constantly. The herd once again appeared against the red-hued sky at dusk, tumbling like a small stream down the sandy slopes of the mountain, arriving in the immense silence that falls over the land just before nightfall. The animals scattered to return to their stables, and Mohand, his job accomplished, disappeared into the small streets, while I had to concentrate on my homework. I don't know what happened to this friend with the earthy scent of a shepherd, a strong-bodied boy of few words and the keen eyes of a watchman. We went our separate ways. Between age-old traditions and a modern path, I don't know which one of us had a better life, but I have carried a tenacious and painful nostalgia throughout my entire life about this time. I have often regretted not becoming a free shepherd in the desert–but how to know what life holds for each one of us? *Mektoub*: "It is written."

I still envy my nomadic ancestors who wandered across the desert with their livestock and their camels. A fleeting people, living everywhere and nowhere, they roamed over the rocky ground and dunes of sand. They appeared and disappeared into the vast horizons and the horizontal chasm of the immense desert. The frugality required by their lifestyle made them a free people. Carrying anything superfluous meant additional weight, which is incompatible with an incessantly itinerant life spent journeying across infinite spaces.

I also see the image of my grandmother, who through some unknown magic, was able to transform desert plants, a few handful of grains, and a bit of milk from her two slender goats into a banquet. Her home was nothing more than a tarp strung up in the night sky, in keeping with the pastoral tradition. Everything was simple.

Yet freedom is not entirely carefree, as death can appear at any time. Leaving behind the superfluous brings into clear focus that which is necessary and essential. Woe to nomads who, in addition to the precious sustenance contained in their leather bags, forget the bucket and rope to draw water, *the* essential substance in this sweltering land, the realm of thirst. They also need to be able to light fires and respond to medical emergencies, especially snake bites. They obviously have to be able to navigate flawlessly, guided by the constellations and the landmarks etched into an infallible memory transmitted from generation to generation. This culture, shared by all nomadic people on the planet, is dedicated to the power of frugality; and I must admit some pride in the art of my ancestors, a combination of strength, patience, endurance, and lightheartedness.

In this frugal world, hospitality is a moral and spiritual rule, as it is among so many traditional people. Many visitors, returning from so-called "poor" countries, describe the hospitality they received from the local people, where the precariousness of their lives does not absolve them from demonstrating generosity to strangers. Their guiding principle: the abundance of any person or family is meant to be shared. "God gives, so that we, too, may give."

The art of living together

The point of all these stories is not to conjure up some kind of nostalgia for an ideal, bygone world, but to regret that it has not been given its due, that its positive values have not been merged with our contemporary world, rather than abolished. We must be wary of glorifying the past and the myth of the "noble savage." Wherever humans have existed, there have been torment and its impact: violence, jealousy, and worse. Traditions also encompass practices and behavior that can shock us. Yet it would be unfair to use this as a pretext to ignore elements within these traditions that honor the individual and the values that the world needs now more than ever.

Traditional cultures that practice moderation probably inherited an ancient vision by which humans felt that they belonged to life rather than claiming to own it. The cultures that developed after the Neolithic Revolution introduced the concept of stockpiling, nearly always abandoning the principle of moderation. To become more settled and to acquire more power, they instituted a policy of extensive rapaciousness, always "seeking more": more land for agriculture and livestock; and more wood for housing, shipbuilding, metalwork, pottery, charcoal, limestone, wars. The amount of resources taken by the newly "civilized" peoples was always exorbitant compared with that of traditional populations. From using resources to meet legitimate needs and the basic necessities of life, we have acquired an irrepressible drive to "possess." Need we recall that certain civilizations, now beloved by archaeologists who decipher their petrified memories, were buried under the sands of the deserts they created? In a way, the principle of economic growth originated with this type of behavior. We left behind guiding principles that knew nothing of dissipation, that were crucial to the sustainability of resources, in favor of one that depletes these same resources, a process undertaken by the greediest people, to the detriment of a considerable number of their fellow humans. Thus was created the principle in inequality and inequity that we deplore today. The rules of temperance have been replaced by those of greed. Instead of the earth as a place of life, we have the earth as a deposit of mineral, plant, and animal resources, to be pillaged without restraint. Meanwhile, the natural context–in other words, the entire planetary ecosystem–would have us moderate our needs to promote a true economy working on behalf of humanity and with respect for all living organisms. What we now call "economy" has become the subtle art of redefining predatory behavior as a science; its complexity perpetuates the considerable role of all things superfluous, while a traditional mode of life would instead be an optimal way of living together in utter simplicity.

Even within an inhospitable environment, like scorching deserts or icy expanses, humans have demonstrated an ability to maximize the available resources, however meager they may be. Many populations on the planet have achieved this balance in their relationship with the natural world. Once again, this is not meant to idealize these cultures to the point of overlooking their less admirable aspects–even though precepts dictated by a moral code required by communal life could moderate negative impulses, and charismatic leaders could help to maintain harmony within the group. With serenity and a light heart, we can always construct a given way of life, anywhere and anytime, if we truly choose to do so. But can we achieve this goal in our encumbered world, cluttered with so many superfluous elements? Our uncertain future will certainly inspire the innovations necessary to continue our story.

4. Connecting with the sacred nature of life

I am no longer a member of any religion–although I owe them for the awareness of transcendence–but I have come to realize that the power of restraint, for me, falls decisively within a mystical and spiritual realm. Because of the inner clarity it creates, it becomes a place of freedom, free from all the torments created by the weight of our everyday lives.

Is there life after death? To this eternal question, raised since humans became sentient creatures, there is no definitive response, other than faith, held as fact by believers. We have only theories, and the debates raised by this impossible question will continue ad infinitum. Everyone finds the answer that best suits them, adheres to their own beliefs, or accepts doubt, skepticism, atheism. Some religions were wise enough from the beginning to proclaim that God Himself was inexpressible: the One about whom we cannot speak. Unfortunately, library shelves are groaning under the weight of contradictory and even conflicting arguments concerning this principle of ineffability. Once again, silence is the only realistic response to this immeasurable mystery that we call life. Despite our wild imaginings, and despite the beauty of our planet and our creative intelligence, we have to admit that neither religion nor art, science, politics, or philosophy have brought peace to the world, our hearts, or our spirits. It's possible that our world would be even more barbaric without these factors, but I can't help thinking that they have also been elements of dissension and violence.

It's a shame that the time spent trying to determine whether there is life after death is not instead devoted to comprehending what life is, understanding its immense value, and working to make it a masterpiece inspired by a vibrant and active humanism, where restraint would be a true mode of existence. It would be a shame, after so much suffering and absurdity, to wonder, at the end of one's own life, not whether there is life after death, but rather if there is life before death, and what this represents in the great mystery of life itself. Is an accomplished existence measured in terms of economic and political success, or something else? Everything in this eventful stream that we call history is ephemeral. Even those we recognize as "great human beings" disappear, leaving in the depths of our memories nothing more than a fleeting trace in the infinite immensity of silence. All the scientific disciplines together cannot enlighten us, because they only provide us with fragments of a phenomenon that eludes overall comprehension. For humble spirits, however, they do serve to illustrate the impossibility of limited thought to provide access to a reality that is infinite by nature. When the mind becomes aware of its limitations, we reach the limits of the unknown. And this is a place of calm, of restraint, leading us to a sense of contemplation free of useless doubts, expectations, or ambition, while our deepest selves become receptive to that which is expressible in any language. The silence in response to our desire to understand the essence of the essential may be the root of our greatest torments, transforming our lives into prisons, even though the entire universe offers the greatest possible freedom. Our knowledge may have been able to explain how a single seed germinates and perpetuates life, but it has never elucidated the "why" of life itself.

Truth is not something to be flushed out somewhere. No philosophy, no dogma or precept, no ideology can capture it, even less put it in a cage. It appears only once we stop speculating and torturing ourselves. We can apprehend it in silence and immobility, where there is no room for a viewpoint, no opinion on what cannot be explained. Truth seems to preexist everything else that exists. I believe that this is probably what we call the power of the divine–a rather intuitive guess shadowed by permanent doubt–which our distant ancestors, primitive mankind, could sense in every manifestation of life.

4

IN SUPPORT OF RESTRAINT

1. Poverty as a measure of well-being

This is the title of a chapter from my autobiography published in 1984, on the insistence of a friend, a small publisher in the Ardèche. I had named this short work *Du Sahara aux Cévennes* (From the Sahara to the Cévennes), and to avoid any confusion with a sort of "Paris-Dakar" race in reverse, I added a subtitle, *Ou la Reconquête du Songe* (Or recapturing the dream). Symbolically, it meant recapturing freedom from time and money constraints to rediscover the aimless timelessness of a dream.

The concept of poverty was unsettling, but it was a genuine life choice for us, not just another moral statement. My unswerving conviction that the future lies in a civilization of restraint was growing stronger, and becoming, with the unbridled consumerism gripping the world, a vital necessity.

I would like to support my remarks with actual experience, which represents our state of mind as early as 1961, when we decided to give up city life for nature and live off the land. *Du Sahara aux Cévennes*, which many readers know for its prediction of some developments that characterize our society today, describes the journey of a small Saharan boy, born into a traditional Muslim family. For utmost clarity, I have borrowed some of my experiences and included them in this book. I hope the reader will not see this as an exercise in vanity, but rather as facts to support the subject at hand, the power of restraint.

My mother died when I was four years old, and my father, a blacksmith, entrusted me to a childless French couple so that I could be educated. As a child, it was very difficult for me to deal with the fact of belonging to two cultures, often with contradictory values. Between tradition and modernity, Islam and Christianity, the northern and southern hemispheres, I grew up far from my traditional family, as my adoptive family had been transferred to northern Algeria.

I did not do well in school, but later I became an irrepressible autodidact. I wanted to understand, to find answers. I studied history and read philosophers, humanists, and mystics. I converted to Catholicism at the age of sixteen. In the midst of all these changes, I began to wonder about the basis of this civilization that taught me my ancestors were the Gauls. As an adolescent, I also suffered from the violence of the Algerian War of Independence. I finally left Algeria for France in the late 1950s, absolutely alone. I found a job as a skilled worker in the Paris region and realized fairly quickly that I could not subscribe to a model of society that clearly alienated the individuals within it. I met Michèle, and together we decided to start a family, but not in this uprooted world. In 1961, driven by a desire to get back to nature, we moved to the Cévennes hills in the Ardèche region of France.

We did not have a penny to purchase land on which we could build our dream; the only possibility, recommended by some supportive friends, was to take out a loan with the Crédit Agricole, which was still operating like a true mutual bank. The branch in Vans, in the southern Ardèche, informed us that we needed to have some training as farmers to acquire a loan. Perfectly logical, but I had to admit that I did not have the required qualifications. To meet this condition, I took basic agriculture classes on a family farm in the Ardèche countryside. The courses cost money and as our resources were extremely limited, I had to double down in order to assimilate the three-year program in just one year. I earned my Brevet d'Aptitude Agricole (BAA, agricultural competency certificate), which I completed with two years as a field laborer.

After traveling throughout the region on my scooter looking for an available farm, I finally found a place that captivated both Michèle and myself, and we decided to move there. With the cadastral plan in hand and hope in my heart, I went to the Crédit Agricole branch to submit my request. But the branch manager was distressed with the description of the land. The ten acres dry, rocky garigue consisted of small plots eked out by several generations of farmers doggedly clearing rocks. The stone farmhouse was still standing in the middle of the austere land, but was in need of some fairly major renovation work. No more than 40 cubic yards of rainwater were stored in tanks fashioned from natural underground formations by earlier inhabitants.

The bank officer thought our choice was so unrealistic that he said he didn't want to help us kill ourselves by granting us our loan. This was a time of a massive rural exodus, with a correspondingly high number of abandoned farms, as illustrated by the list the director showed me: his finger slid down the sheet of paper and stopped at a 100-acre farm in the fertile plain of the Eyrieux Valley, a paradise for fruit trees in general, and the famous Ardèche peach in particular. He said: "I would rather loan you 400,000 francs to purchase this farm where you 'will make money,' rather than 15,000 for a place where clearly you and your family will perish." Out of my mouth, as if I were inebriated, sprang words that I would immediately regret: "Sir, I am not interested in money"–something you should never say to a banker. He didn't say a word, but his discouraged look and the way he put away his list spoke volumes about his exasperation, which in hindsight I completely understand. As my request could not merely be ignored, we filled out the papers and submitted our file to the bank's selection and approval commission. In the meantime, the interchange with the branch director ended with a curt goodbye and I left the establishment in a state of utmost confusion. I felt as if, by giving in to a sincere, but stupid impulse, I had committed a blunder that would be fatal to my project, a blunder for which I paid with days and nights of worry and insomnia.

How could I have explained to this person, who truly viewed us in good faith, that our project–although it certainly included the need to make money–also had other goals? How to make this man, who was entirely devoted to the ideology of agricultural productivism, that the beauty of the site, the silence that surrounded it, the light, and the magnificent landscape were priceless to us? Indeed, so much so that they were decisive factors, despite the most unfavorable agronomical conditions. We merely wanted to live from the produce grown on this land, as well as the intangible nourishment offered in such abundance by nature, demanding nothing in return yet yielding so much inner satisfaction. finally, thanks to support from a senator who understood our aspirations, we were able to obtain a two-percent loan over twenty years, which was essentially a gift. And that is how we acquired this property, where we have been living for forty-five years.

While it may have seemed preposterous in an era marked by the effervescence and prosperity of the "Trente Glorieuses," we had just deliberately and consciously opted for "the power of restraint" as a lifestyle choice. Paradoxically, this move toward simplicity involved restrictions and complications of all sorts, which sometimes pushed us to the limits of our endurance. Even simplicity, in a world devoted to unchecked profit, has a cost. But with this quest, we felt we were on a liberating and true path, intimately connected to a nature whose beauty and mystery filled our sprits with the sense of being truly linked to a fundamental essence and its boundless energy. We were immersed in it; this is how, through the force of our convictions, we had the courage to transform a stark, austere place into a humble oasis, a small realm of patience.

We survived on our meager reservoirs for seven years, while waiting for the municipal water supply to be extended to the house. We didn't have electricity for thirteen years: candles, petrol lamps, and gas lamps sufficed. After it rained, our trusty old Juva 4–which I worked on assiduously until it finally gave up the ghost–could not climb the dirt road leading to the house. In short, modern comfort had not yet arrived to this enclave; its integrity reflected a bygone era, toward which I still feel a tug of nostalgia.

Ecological principles govern our methods for managing this small domain, to the exclusion of any harmful chemicals. This is based on a radical refusal of the precepts of industrial agriculture, which cannot produce without destroying, which for us is a major assault on the earth, nature, and human beings. Pesticides affect every branch of natural life, including people through the adulterated food we eat. This is why we adopted an ecological life, joining forces with the very few dedicated pioneers in organic and ecological farming. The agronomical methods used on our property have been tested on other sites, notably in the Sahel regions that suffered so seriously during the droughts of the 1970s. The farmer without borders had become a small warrior, an advocate for the land; respect for this nature is the greatest opportunity given to us to delight in life, rather than becoming destructive predators. The process became a commitment and an initiation into the great mysteries.

The principle of restraint I support is not just an improvised plan; it is based on a conviction that is intrinsically linked to a life choice. We never considered the domestic animals and the magnificent land that supported us as a means for earning the money that we, like everyone else, needed. We viewed them as offerings, over and beyond mere resources we exploited to meet our physical needs. Along the way, we did experience financial concerns, inner conflicts, dissent, and differences, but these difficulties were ultimately necessary to reaching a better understanding of ourselves and of others. This life is clearly an upward-moving rite of passage. As we climbed, as if on the slopes of a mountain of uncertainty, ignorance, and doubt, the landscape opened up before us, grew more intelligible, while our awareness was heightened and became clearer.

This singular path–constructing a structured living space, and reconciling economic demands with ecological concerns–required a great deal of rigor. Living an alternate lifestyle within a society firmly based on principles established as irrevocable standards raised a number of questions that we were not always prepared to tackle.

By "rigor" I mean how seriously we worked to construct an alternative—although not to the point of crippling rigidity—using whatever means we had available and others we invented, especially when money was lacking. Advances made by revolutionary protest movements, as in 1968, have often been dashed or reduced to a bare minimum, when irreverence was mistaken for freedom, itself equated with a refusal of any constraints. A rational and objective vision is essential to meeting material needs. We therefore managed our little farm as a small company, complying with the necessary administrative rules. But, as opposed to what occurs in an ordinary company, where growth is synonymous with success, we opted for voluntary restraint from the start. This was the key to our success, because restraint is indeed a force. The value added to basic products was based on a marketing relationship that included a social factor: friendly interchanges and dialogue at the markets and on the farm. We avoided becoming marginalized at all costs, cutting ourselves off from the community around us. For us, living an alternate lifestyle did not mean building an enclave within this community. Restraint as a principle of life and restraint as an inner experience are two sides of the same coin, representing the same search for meaning and coherence.

2. Voluntary restraint

I have to admit that after a period of frugality that sometimes bordered on indigence, which my family experienced for some fifteen years during the pioneering phase of our Cévennes adventure beginning in 1961, we now enjoy a reasonable, but hard-fought prosperity. And I have to ask myself: what exactly is this restraint that I advocate? Is my life still consistent with our initial choice, especially given that the serious crisis now facing our societies reinforces its relevance and urgency–given that after years spent living without, I now enjoy most of the attributes of modern life and the ensuing expensive lifestyle?

I do not have a yacht or a private jet, which I neither need nor want, but this modest prosperity has allowed us–in addition to the immense privilege of living amid this magnificent nature–to benefit from most of the innovations derived from this famous "progress" intended to improve the human condition. I am therefore immersed in a situation whose very principles I oppose, where the limit between restraint and non-restraint has become totally blurred.

While roundly condemning any exploitation of individuals, I have to admit that despite my relatively moderate environmental footprint, I am a capitalist. For confirmation, I just have to visit a village in Africa's Sahel region where we have been pursuing agroecology initiatives; there, I am a millionaire. For the price of my mid-range car, which I definitely need as a means of transport, filled with books and documents for my conferences, an African village of two hundred people could cover their food costs for at least two years, if they purchased rather than produced it. And if I added up my few possessions and annual expenses, the disparity would be stark indeed. The system is organized so that if we were to take the most legitimate basic needs as a baseline in the hierarchy of possessions, we would come up with far more capitalists.

It's fair to say that once essential needs have been met, indexed to a basic level of survival that includes food, fresh water, shelter, clothing, health care for all–which are far from being met worldwide–we enter the sphere of the superfluous, marked by unfair and unlimited accumulation.

If we take a closer look at the overall organization, or rather disorganization, by which the necessary goods for survival are distributed, voluntary restraint would automatically generate fairness. Until every person has access to basic resources, if the goal on this shared planet is to create an equal, just place inspired by moral principles, we have to speak of plunder. As long as any children are born without what they legitimately deserve, their rights have been usurped, because the goods on this still abundant earth are meant for all creatures, not merely for those who, through political power, the laws of the marketplace, finance, and weapons, have claimed ownership. This theft has been sanctioned by laws establishing standards that we can no longer challenge. Until this dishonesty is viewed as illicit, according to the order and intelligence of life, humanity will not be able to survive.

Misery, poverty, and wealth coexist on our planet, creating hierarchies of possessions and power that lead to all kinds of repression– and we can lay the blame squarely on the ideology of unlimited acquisition. Would the famous "purchasing power" have any meaning without the reigning rationale, which reduces the individual to the status of mere consumer? Lessening enthusiasm for consumerism is logically viewed as harmful to the system. Consuming, with all the inherent risk of physic and physical obesity, has become something of a civic duty, based on a reverse sense of asceticism, in which insatiability and dissatisfaction form alternating poles of the economy. Gratitude, moderation, and balance are the sentiments and virtues that *Homo economicus*, mere gears in an immense global machine, must abolish at all cost, as they are dangerous to the metabolism of the pseudo-economy that is gripping the world by its throat.

Once again, how to clearly define what "restraint" should be in such a complicated context? Especially because without social aid from governments and charitable organizations, an even larger number of people in the so-called developed world would be living in an unbearable state of poverty. This situation leads families directly into over-indebtedness, to which is added the debts of countries and those of an ever-increasing number of public institutions. A situation that no one dares call a "recession" is no less a reality for not being named. Given the pseudo-economic mechanisms that govern the relationships among nations and the costly, if not to say sumptuous operation of states, this situation can only result in a domino effect of bankruptcies among nations. Social palliatives and containment will be powerless to check an irreversible phenomenon that governs the rules of national and international cohabitation. This situation necessarily destroys the ability to maintain an economy first through work and then through purchasing power.

Compassionate solidarity will come to an end, without any idea of what could replace it. There's no point in producing goods to sell while excluding a large number of people who cannot acquire them. The politics of the pyromaniac fireman unfortunately releases states from any responsibility toward citizens who have mandated them to govern the collective fate of their nations. The failures and incompetence of the system are such that increasingly violent and uncontrollable rebellions are sure to increase if global governance insists on maintaining an inhumane framework that produces suffering and indifference.

For the hardest hit, the principle of restraint obviously makes no sense and could legitimately be interpreted as provocation or mockery. Compassionate solidarity is clearly insufficient for people whose legitimate right to exist has been usurped, taking away the right to self-sufficiency and responsibility that society must ensure for everyone. Restraint, in this case, is a factor of justice and equality, but it necessarily means giving up the current model, which is based on the omnipotence of money and devotion to it. We can never overstate that nothing is possible without renouncing this model. An objective observation of the facts reveals the absolute necessity of a paradigm that positions humans and nature–along with the economy and all its resources–at the heart of our concerns.

I am often asked what I mean by this "power of restraint" that I promote as a sort of antidote to the rut of the joyless, overabundant society of developed countries. Beyond the aesthetic, seductive, and poetic aspects, this idea resonates with me as a necessity inspired by an analysis of quantifiable and objective facts, which strongly determine the future. I had adopted by term "sustainable degrowth," coined by the Romanian economist Nicholas Georgescu-Roegen. I made it a central tenet of my pre-electoral campaign for the 2002 presidential elections in France, but had to give it up, as this term is often misconstrued. Yet I did not give up the economic premises and analysis developed Roegen, which are still extremely relevant. For this unusual economist, the only worthwhile economy is one that produces well-being with restraint. This belief been obvious to me for a long time, as I have already said.

The array of issues discussed with such clarity by Roegen will eventually prevail, simply because they are realistic. Given the speed at which a minority with an unshakeable belief in unlimited growth and ever more finance is using up resources, the rate of depletion is rising at an exponential rate. By opting for a developmental model leading to disaster, emerging countries are contributing to an accelerating process that can only be fatal to the human species. Must we keep repeating this over and over again? We cannot apply an artificially unlimited principle to a planet that is naturally limited. Concurrent with our task of re-enchanting the world–as beauty is clearly an absolutely essential, intangible nourishment for our evolution to a genuine humanism–we must also find a fair way of living on the planet by matching our destiny to it in a way that is satisfying to the heart, spirit, and mind. By beauty I mean that which is expressed through generosity, fairness, and respect. It alone can change the world, as it is more powerful than all the beauty created by the hand of mankind–which, as prolific as it may be, has not and will not ever save the world. In truth, our survival depends on it. The choice of a way of life based on collective and individual self-restraint is crucial; this is a fact.

3. Human change

During my electoral campaign for the 2002 French presidential elections, I stressed–and continue to stress–that the destructive model of society that rules the entire world cannot be patched back together again. A blind insistence on maintaining it, as world governments are doing, is useless and will only prolong its death throes. The disastrous effects are only increasing in scale. The geopolitical changes required for a new world order are incompatible with the principle of unlimited economic growth. Climate, ecological, economic, and social change, both predictable and unpredictable, require an unprecedented degree of creativity. Starting with individual choices about lifestyles, we are now compelled to work on restraint for the entire world. By shifting from a rationale of unlimited profit to that of living organisms, the question then becomes one of "changing the paradigm."

Placing the priority on people and nature

Restructuring the future based on the natural world first requires giving up the founding myths of the modern age, which are incompatible with this path. Restraint, if it prevails, will certainly be a tremendous antidote to destructive excess. Changing the paradigm means placing a priority on people and nature and using every possible means to support them. We find ourselves dreaming of summit meetings involving every nation, finally acknowledging that planet earth is not a giant source of raw materials to be depleted, but a precious oasis for life. The most essential goods must be protected by specific regulations. Radical resolutions must be voted in to preserve its integrity. The forests, soil, water, seeds, and fishery resources, among others, must be exempt from all financial speculation. It is disheartening and distressing to see humanity's essential heritage, and the countless creatures that share our destiny, rendered shamelessly subservient to the vulgarity of finance.

> *Only once the last tree is cut, the last river poisoned, the last fish captured, only then will you discover that you cannot eat money.*

This prophecy is pure intelligence, that of traditional, indigenous peoples. Protecting these people, these vulnerable and innocent witnesses against the arbitrary actions and wickedness of so-called civilized people must be a priority, protected by strict laws. In addition to direct atrocities are the genocides caused by the confiscation and destruction of their natural environments, with which they have co-existed in a perfect symbiosis since the dawn of time. The environments must also be viewed as common goods that they have been able to preserve; and for that, we should be grateful to them. The abuse and contempt they have suffered border on cowardice and constitute the gravest form of offense against humanity.

Over-romanticizing them is probably not fair. These communities also have their imperfections, and behaviors that need changing. I am often shocked by the diminished role reserved to women. Through their deeply held convictions and their lifestyles, however, these people, who are still strongly linked to the basic elements of life, can teach us that it is possible to achieve harmony between the human species and nature. Their right to exist on their lands, according to their own values that give meaning to their lives, as it does to each and every one of us, is utterly legitimate. Our commitment in support of this right must not be distorted by pity or condescension. Their lifestyles and their messages help awaken us to the sacred nature of life.

Rebalancing feminine and masculine energies

The myth of man as demiurge as a masculine concept—one particularly glorified by the technological culture—is confirmed by the absence of female participation in this culture. The most compelling example of feminine energy as a guardian force of life that I have seen took place in the Sahel. Harvests in the 1980s had been destroyed by drought, producing severe food shortages. In these circumstances, the impotence of the human species borders of humiliation. The men, thrown into total disarray, were forced to look for work elsewhere—or used this pretext as a reason to flee. The women, responsible for the children, deployed an unbelievable level of energy, seemingly heightened and sharpened, rather than sapped, by the exhausting situation. Hard-working groups would go into the desert, battling for hours a type of grass—cram-cram—that stuck to their clothes with small hooks to laboriously eke out a few seeds to survive. The extreme ordeal over which these destitute women triumphed moved me profoundly, and inspired a short invocation of gratitude: "We should perhaps ask one last act of courage from the women responsible for the water, the fire, the land, and life, to climb up to the great sacred eminences and offer to the dusk what remains of our fervor so that tomorrow, there will be light."

We are constantly discussing the tragedy represented by the universal subordination of the feminine energy. The new rationale cannot retain a stance toward this problem bordering on fatalism, which is at the root of our history's imbalance. It is urgent to acknowledge the absolute necessity of rebalancing the masculine/feminine energies, starting with our children's education. The issue is not about some politically correct parity, but a dynamic harmonization and rapprochement of values and talents, creating a complementarity that could save the world.

The image of women in modern society is something like a raw material with high added value with all kinds of marketable fantasies.

Every single newsstand has shelves full of half-nude women, reduced to mere commodities; indeed, the sexual attributes of women are used as ubiquitous selling points for any number of products. These images propel sales according to subliminal processes that act on both men and women, based on humiliating portrayals and a huge dose of mental manipulation, a sphere in which advertising excels. The budgets for these campaigns are then factored into the costs of the beauty products themselves, accounting for no small share of the price. Furthermore, the condition of women in various cultures, the historical dependence on men as protectors, the legal and moral codification that confirmed this dependency may play a role in the quest for security through seduction. Some women feel they have to conform to these arbitrary rules even though they don't need the "security." In addition, shop windows, magazines, and advertising are all ways to escape and to fill a social and emotional void. Need we bring up the significant fact that throughout the world, women had to wait many long years before getting the right to vote. It is not just because a democracy has finally declared equality between the sexes that this equality is manifested in real life. A quasi-indestructible male chauvinism remains embedded in the deepest part of the male psyche.

If we add the effects of ageing, often experienced as a loss of seductive power, it then becomes hard to resist the lure of anything that could provide a fix. And yet how many elderly women who have passed the age of objective aesthetic criteria, of artificial codes and canons, have an inner beauty, an unalterable charm that is profoundly moving. Being handsome or beautiful, in keeping with the different criteria of various cultures, is a universal need. Among the poor in many countries, male and female elegance exists at all ages, but at a very low cost. Elegance, charm, and beauty are not incompatible with restraint and are not dependent on large sums of money. This is indeed a fascinating subject of reflection and meditation.

Teaching the individual

A change in mentalities cannot occur without a total reassessment of children's education. The current system is inspired and determined by the priorities of a financial and commercial ideology, and a passive surrender to a teaching caste. We are well aware of the extreme importance of the context surrounding the conception, gestation, and birth of a child. Enough with the hypocrisy: what everyone calls "education" is a machine to produce soldiers for the pseudo-economy, not fulfilled human beings who can think, analyze, create, and master their emotions as well as what we call spirituality. "Educating," at least in France, is essentially the act of crushing children to reformat them to a conformist mold. The increasing malaise of an entire generation of young people heading for failure when the system cannot make room for them or take responsibility for them reflects this alienation. The prevailing formula, particularly during the "Trente Glorieuses," by which a good education was a guarantee of a good salary, is no longer true in a society of unlimited growth. Why, then, cling stubbornly to this already obsolete option?

In the new paradigm, we must place a priority on children, by developing a teaching method for individuals that promotes self-fulfillment, in other words, one that helps children discover their own unique personality and talents, discover a direction that provides meaning to their existence in society and the world. It is by developing an inner coherence that children acquire the sense of having a genuine role to play in a diverse world. For this self-fulfillment to actually occur, it is crucial to abolish the unbearable climate of competition that makes every child fell like the world is a physical and psychic stadium, producing an anxiety of failure at the expense of an enthusiasm for learning.

The overwhelming importance accorded the intellect to the detriment of manual intelligence, to which we owe our evolution, is a catastrophe that has disabled us, unknowingly. It has created a sort of arbitrary hierarchy that offers keys to decision-making processes that are untested by any tangible experience. A direct relationship with nature is also essential; this is a lifelong bond to which children owe their lives. It is crucial to understand this vital principle; not doing so would be a monumental lapse.

Education must restore a balance among different subjects and abilities. Schools should all offer gardening options, introductory workshops in manual activities, and art classes. Organic gardens would provide tangible experience of the intangible laws of living organisms: the fertility of the earth, its generosity in offering the food we need, and the mystery and beauty of the phenomena that govern the huge complexity of what we call ecology. School should also be a place to teach children about the feminine/masculine complementarity; educating them about restraint can also be a decisive lesson for their entire lives. Children in consumerist societies, who know nothing about the process of producing the goods they use so abundantly in our culture of overabundance, and the fate of the waste they produce down the line, are reduced to the sad function of small, wasteful consumers. They are unaware of their contribution to the collective excess of the wealthy and their joyless privileges, while so many children continue to live in countries where their daily lives are stamped with frugality–if not outright poverty. Paradoxically, I have often observed in the eyes of these children a brightly burning spark, as if hope remains strong, despite everything. An introduction to restraint is a source of joy, as it leads more easily to satisfaction, eliminating the frustration produced by evermore desire, a state maintained by disturbingly successful advertising–from which all children should be protected. This hostage situation produces jaded, disillusioned children, displaying an attitude of "everything, right now." Patience, and the ensuing sense of value and meaning, would put an end to this desire. Along the same lines, the toy industry contributes to adult interference in children's imaginations. Saturated with ready-to-use educational tools and games, children are diverted from their natural ability to create their own games and toys with an incomparable degree of inventiveness. This creativity, accentuated by their candor, contributes strongly to the concept of restraint in that it eliminates the extravagant proliferation of objects that use up raw materials, often derived from oil, as well as energy, pollution, recycling, and so on.

Furthermore, the exorbitant number of toys that convey detrimental and perverse symbols of contemporary society is highly regrettable. They instill the toxins of depravity into innocent souls: violence, murder, pornography, etc. Governments and parents must urgently lay down strict rules to protect children, who are so vulnerable and easy to manipulate, from desires that jeopardize their integrity. This problem does not need a moralistic or convenient Manichean response, but rather an objective reply to an objective situation, provided by the adults who are responsible for the future of the generations entrusted to them. It is not enough to ask: "What planet will we leave our children?"; we must also ask ourselves: "What kind of children will we leave to our planet?"

The condition of our elders

This inventory of major aspects of the current human condition must include that of our elderly, a situation that is harmful to both the heart and mind. No one can escape the condition of ageing. Such is life: youth is nothing but ephemeral in this merry-go-round we are on. Yet organized society is based on a *Homo economicus* viewed as a productive and consuming entity, the two pistons in the motor of the pseudo-economy. In this context, ageing is not about fulfillment, being productive, and transmitting to the future before passing away, but rather slowly declining before disappearing altogether. It is not surprising, under these conditions, that a fear of ageing should be so widespread. The very organization of urban life, which is increasingly inhuman, is incompatible with the age-old mutual assistance among generations within an extended family situation. Solidarity that has become streamlined by social policies such as retirement, social security, and other benefits, is already overextended. In France, the social welfare system provides health, housing, education, and unemployment benefits to people in need. Everyone knows that these measures depend on the creation of financial wealth. When this wealth diminishes or even disappears, as is entirely possible, they will necessarily disappear in turn.

Retired people today enjoy benefits that put them in a paradoxically privileged position, provided they have sufficient retirement funds. Some of them use these benefits to support children and grandchildren, who are sometimes unemployed despite their youthful energy and lengthy preparation to enter what is known by the detestable expression as the "job market." This imbalance is one of the major signs pointing to the decline of the dominant context, a factor contributing to social chaos. A sober analysis of this situation reveals that the elderly, with the resources they are given and the care that they require, are bleeding the system dry. They are canvased by politicians for their votes and courted by travel agents and banks that want their savings, but what will happen once the money has been dissipated?

The elderly must dread the prospect of their later years, condemned to isolation, to the solitude of a sterile world. Communities have always factored in the need for continuity, the transmission of the knowledge acquired over a long life of experience from elders to a younger generation. It is wonderful to see a child and a senior walking and chatting together. They represent the two extremes of life, its coherence and cyclical nature. Our era, which has partitioned ages and life passages, has added to the pain of an end-of-life situation.

Regardless of what we do, keeping an entire nation alive through palliative measures is a limited option. Political governance, caught in its own contradictions, its sterile quarrels, its electrical timetables, polls and popularity ratings, cannot–or will not–looks clearly and objectively at the reality. It merely provides substitute social measures, as a sort of institutionalized handout–while awaiting what? Added to this is the assistance provided by charitable institutions– United Way, Salvation Army, Feeding America, Goodwill, Catholic Relief Services, among many others–whose roles are on the rise. Not to mention the subsidies granted to farmers and the myriad of small NGOs working to fix collateral failures. We admire and are grateful for all these heartfelt efforts, but unfortunately they let governments off the hook, so that they are not responsible, by concealing the symptoms that could lead to a more realistic diagnosis and inspire radical decisions equal to the urgency of the task at hand.

A major social storm seems to be brewing, given the extreme poverty of many people and the ensuing frustration and indignation toward the sometimes ostentatious arrogance of the very wealthy, to arbitrary political action, excessive vanity, the dumbing-down of the population in general, and countless acts of manipulation. It is impossible to draw up a comprehensive list of all the damage inflicted on mankind by mankind. Similarly, the suffering inflicted by humans on all living creatures, whose only mistake is to exist on this planet at the same time as us, does not seem to affect either our consciences or our hearts. Need we repeat that over millennia, we have amassed a debt toward animals, the companions of our destiny? What would the Inuit be without the dogs and the Arctic fauna on which they depend? The Bedouins without their dromedaries? The Laplanders without reindeer? And elsewhere, in other environments, the camel, the yack, the draft horse, the ox, the buffalo? What ingratitude. The contemporary world has eliminated entire swaths of animal biodiversity, both in the wild and among domestic species. It inflicts suffering on animals that even the most basic morality cannot deny; or idolizes them to the point of folly, in which the everyday lives of animals have very little in common with their true natures. During an agroecology workshop, it was difficult for me to convince the African students that the amount of money spent on pets in rich countries was greater than the national budgets of certain so-called developing countries. In the quest for restraint, this, too, is another subject that deserves further consideration. Regardless of the sector of modern life we examine, it is clear that we are always on the far end of the spectrum in terms of restraint. So much waste, such lavish and useless spending by countries!

It is safe to say that as long as omnipresent, omnipotent, and omni-stultifying money continues to be a pernicious fluid trickling through people's mind, dehumanizing and destroying any sense of restraint, the human species will not only be unable to evolve, but will regress. It would be singularly naïve, hypocritical, and ignorant to believe that the small and large international conferences on carbon issues and other pretexts will produce any positive, intelligent story. The fact is, intelligence has nothing to do with the countless skills we have acquired. The fragmented vision of reality; the excessive specialization; the impressive number of scientific, technical and medical disciplines; and the multiple institutes and other academies have not only not saved the world, but have sometimes hastened its decline. It's important to stop looking at the past with such a condescending view and try to make good use of the best that it has produced. This past must be viewed as a legacy of humanity to be rehabilitated and incorporated into the positive aspects of contemporary life, which has been privatized, taken hostage by the profit motive. But all this must be driven by intelligence, in other words, lucidity, which is not about a well-oiled, high-functioning brain, but implies a connection to a transcendent order that predates our appearance on earth and to which we owe, beyond the shadow of a doubt, our existence. Understanding this order, working with it rather than against it–this is genuine intelligence.

4. A plea for constructive indignation

It is hard not to be outraged by the situation of the world and the direction it has taken. There is a sense of immense waste, avoidable had we adopted a societal model that integrated intelligence and generosity. Outrage has always led to rebellion–which can be effective or toothless, depending on the circumstances. It can also have either the worst or best outcomes; history is littered with multiple examples of both. Some of the most violent dictatorships were established in the wake of legitimate protests against oppression. Unfortunately, the oppressed become the oppressors on achieving power; this will always ensue until every individual has eradicated within themselves the seeds of oppression. Nothing has changed, and while we celebrate walls that come down, others are being built before our eyes, before going up in our hearts. Humanity is versatile and unpredictable, transformed by subjective, uncontrollable mechanisms that call for contemplation; we cannot expect more from humanity than it can give. Throughout the centuries, history has accustomed us to a series of heroes greeted as saviors by cheering crowds, only to be dismissed or even executed when they do not fulfill the often outlandish expectations with which they were tasked–unless they have set themselves up as lifelong authoritarian rulers, establishing illegitimate dynasties. In a world so distorted by cowardice and the blind consent of citizens, there is something pathetic in the eternal quest for the providential leader and the scapegoat. Today, through a perversion of democracy that no longer even shocks public opinion, dictators are enthroned and anointed through parodies of universal suffrage. This is still possible because a network of covert interests manages to nip any indignation in the bud; in the face of this iniquity, we limit our reactions to a few ineffectual protests. Are we therefore off the hook for any responsibility about our own fates and that of the collective body? Fates whose meaning and inevitability often escape our understanding. Action and reaction are the warp and weft of history. To escape this inevitability, can we come up with a rationale that is based neither on the antagonism of oppositions and rivalry, with its multiple forms of violence, nor on a sterile consensus based on the compromises imposed by the supremacy of money, the cause of the greatest disasters on the planet? Given the situation to which the human species has evolved, where current issues and deadlines require decisive options, the answer to this question can no longer be deferred, much less avoided. It's time to know where we want to go and what kind of life we want to live, to give some meaning to our time on earth–it's clear that for now, in light of what our presence in the world has caused to living organisms, it would appear that we are probably just an unfortunate accident.

Humanity has such a need for hope and belief that we are always ready to compromise and often take ill-calculated risks. Given my lifelong commitments, some people have criticized me for not being aggressive enough in my protests. "How do you manage to always remain calm when confronted with the most intolerable situations?" These situations are so numerous that our lives could end up being one continuous state of indignation and a condition of permanent powerlessness.

"Are you optimistic or pessimistic for the future?" Georges Bernanos wrote that the optimist is a happy imbecile and a pessimist a sad imbecile. Society is becoming more and more stress producing, a condition that is increasing in conjunction with the destruction of the biosphere and the indigence caused by the growing greed of the human species. Prophecies worthy of ancient oracles and the most irrational predictions coexist with forecasts and prospects based on the most rigorous scientific data, which themselves generate controversies, skepticism, disbelief, pessimism–or an indestructible faith in a better future. None of this will ever enlighten us until we understand that humans cause all human crises, and that, aside from factors beyond our control, the future will be the one we make of it. Nothing else.

Despite my early and still strong sense of rebellion, my basic nature has never leaned toward violent protest; yet I do not support a passive stance. I understand that indignation can generate legitimate aggravation, which in some cases can be essential for promoting change, provided specific changes are identified and the ultimate goals defined. We have a responsibility to maintain a sense of indignation so as not to let indifference take over or give in to a fatalistic outlook leading to powerlessness–which would be disastrous for our dignity. Instead of opting for a violent rebellion, which can instill a sense of action, indignation has been a stimulus for me, a force inspiring me to find new paths where other types of behavior and other choices are possible, if we believe wholeheartedly in them,

More than ever, I am advocating for an "insurrection of consciences," which I adopted as my electoral slogan. This universal appeal seems to be reaching more and more people now. It could inspire an active political movement, based on the power of restraint as an antidote to the power of money. The creation of a microcosm where we can exercise our free will in total independence is possible and necessary if we are to change the world. We can only escape the tyranny of finance by organizing ourselves so that we do not totally depend on it. To achieve this goal, restraint is an absolute necessity. It is up to us to fully embrace this choice, to create a free, serene and unburdened life. We are delighted to note that many initiatives have begun to flourish naturally nearly everywhere in civil society, embodying this fantastic development. I am meeting more and more young people who say they want to have fulfilling lives rather than merely successful careers, company managers who acknowledge they have achieved social success but have failed on a human level. The question of purpose has therefore shifted in relation to earlier criteria, while the quest for meaning seems to have become a priority among life's commitment. Strongly held aspirations for a simple life are still limited by the rigidity of obsolete institutions and structures that must necessarily incorporate the new developments in contemporary society. It is paradoxical that, even living in a restrained way on a plot of land–the goal of increasing numbers of people–requires a solid financial basis. Must living a simple life be an expensive option? More than ever, we need new policies with a realistic and attentive approach to the major movements that are gaining ground and expanding–not to contain them, which would not work, but to support them. The difficult context worldwide that inspired them means that they are a little more universal every day.

Fortunately, utopias flourish, and even if they are not all successful, they demonstrate strong convictions in support of an alternate world. Yet we have to be wary of exaggerating this impact. There are a considerable number of people who are more or less comfortably settled within the former model and who cannot imagine challenging it. The so-called developed countries do not yet seem to be in a position to understand that they have everything to gain in saving traditional social structures by incorporating the positive aspects of the modern age. The so-called "emerging" countries are racing toward the former model, yearning for it with all the energy created by the myth of success based on a model that has clearly demonstrated its failures. This is why innovative initiatives from "advanced" countries must be viewed as prototypes anticipating what will be universally essential in the future–a future that is, at the very least, impossible to predict. I am aware, by promoting the power of restraint, that I have tackled a complex array of problems. My goal is to try to make sense of it, without any certainty of having achieved it; perhaps the future holds the answer.

In any case, I did not intend to merely discuss general issues; I also want the creative structures inspired by and representing the values and utopias I have constantly supported to be highlighted in this book. In addition to initiatives in France concerning changes inspired by a quest for simplicity and coherence, we can add those achieved abroad, in Sub-Saharan Africa, the Maghreb, and Eastern Europe. We are strongly committed to expanding our scope; to do so, an endowment fund has been created. For further information concerning these various structures, please consult our Colibris website: www.colibris-lemouvement.org.

APPENDICES

1. Beautiful dreams, to scatter for future generations

There were humans whose discernment fostered a sense of respect. They educated their offspring with the following words:
Know that creation does not belong to us, but that we are all its children. Refrain from arrogance of any kind, as the trees and all living creatures are also children of creation.

Live an unburdened life, without any contempt for water, wind, or light. And if you take life for your own, do so with gratitude. When you sacrifice an animal, know that this is life giving to life, and take care that nothing in this gift is squandered. Know how to determine the measure of all things. Make no unnecessary noises; do not kill without need or for pleasure.

Know that the trees and the wind delight in the melody they create together; and that birds, carried by the breeze, are messengers of the sky as much as the earth. Remain very aware when the sky illuminates your path; and when the night brings you together, trust it, because if you have no hate nor enemies, it will lead you to the banks of dawn unharmed, on ships of silence.

May neither time nor age be a burden, as they prepare you for other births, and in your diminished days, if your life was righteous it will give birth to new beautiful dreams, to scatter like seeds for future centuries.

2. International charter for the earth and humanity

**What kind of planet will we leave to our children?
What kind of children will we leave to our planet?**

Planet earth today is the only known oasis of life that exists in our immense sidereal desert. The most realistic, magnificent project of all is to take care of it, respecting its physical and biological integrity, using its resources with restraint, and establishing peace and solidarity among humans, with a respect for all forms of life.

Assessment: earth and humanity are both critically endangered

The myth of unlimited growth

The industrial, high-productivity model on which our modern world is based aims to pursue an ideology of "always more" and a quest for unlimited profit on a planet of limited resources. Resources are acquired through looting, competitiveness, and economic warfare among individuals, corporations, and governments. A model reliant on energy combustion and rapidly depleting oil reserves cannot be applied worldwide.

The all-mighty power of money

With money as the exclusive measure of a nation's prosperity, it has taken control of our collective destiny. Anything without monetary parity has no value; any individual without an income is therefore socially eradicated. Even if money could fulfill every desire, it still cannot provide joy and the sheer happiness of being alive.

The disaster of chemical agriculture

The industrialization of agriculture, with its massive use of chemical fertilizers, pesticides, hybrid seeds, and excessive mechanization, has severely damaged the earth's fertility and traditional farming practices. Unable to produce without destroying, humanity may be facing unprecedented famines.

Humanitarian aid instead of a humanistic approach

Even though natural resources are now sufficient to meet the basic needs of everyone, shortages and poverty continue to grow. Since the world does not run according to humanist values, based on fairness, sharing, and solidarity, we rely on humanitarian aid as a palliative. The scenario of the firefighter as arsonist has become the norm.

Disconnect between mankind and nature

Predominantly urban modern society has built an "uprooted" civilization, disconnected from the realities of natural rhythms, which can only worsen the human condition and the damages inflicted on the earth.

Malnutrition, illness, exclusion, violence, discontent, insecurity, pollution of the soil, water and air, depletion of vital resources, and desertification exist in both the northern and southern hemispheres. These observations affect us deeply, appeal to our sense of responsibility and compel us to act urgently to alter these developments; failing to do so threatens our future and that of generations to come.

Proposals: living and taking care of life

Live the utopia

Utopia is not a pipe dream but a "Neverland" of all that can be envisaged. Given the limits and dead-ends of our mode of existence, a utopia is a driving force for life that can render possible everything we imagine is impossible. The solutions of the future exist in the utopias of the present. We must incarnate the initial utopia within ourselves, because social transformation will not occur unless people themselves change.

The earth and humanism

We acknowledge the earth, the common good of humanity, as the sole guarantor of our life and our survival. Inspired by a sense of positive humanism, we consciously commit ourselves to promoting respect for all life forms and contributing to the well-being and fulfillment of all human beings. finally, we consider beauty, moderation, fairness, gratitude, compassion, and solidarity to be essential in building a sustainable and viable world for all.

The principle of living organisms

We consider that the current prevailing model is unsustainable and that a paradigm shift is essential. It is crucial to place people and nature at the heart of our concerns and to mobilize all our resources and skills on their behalf.

Feminine energy: crucial for change

The subordination of the feminine to an extreme and violent masculine world remains one of the major impediments to the positive evolution of mankind. Women are more likely to protect life than destroy it. We must honor women, as guardians of life, and listen to the feminine that lies within each one of us.

Agroecology

Agriculture is the most essential of all human activities, because without food, people cannot survive. The agroecology we advocate as an ethical way of life and agricultural practice enables people to regain their autonomy, as well as their food safety and security, while renewing and preserving their food-producing heritage.

The power of restraint

When confronted with the "always more" ideology that is destroying the planet for the benefit of a minority, restraint is a conscious choice inspired by reason. It is an art and an ethical way of life, a source of deep satisfaction and well-being. It is a political commitment and an act of resistance in favor of the earth, sharing, and fairness.

Recentering the economy

Producing and consuming locally is an absolute necessity for the safety of people in terms of their basic and legitimate needs. Without entirely excluding complementary trading situations, territories would become autonomous homelands promoting and caring for their local resources. Human-scale agriculture, handicrafts, and small businesses should be rehabilitated so that the maximum number of citizens can once again be involved in the economy.

An alternative approach to education

We wish, with all our hearts and minds, for an educational system that is not based on a fear of failure but an enthusiasm to learn. An education that abolishes the concept of "every man for himself" in favor of the power of solidarity and complementarity; that uses everyone's talents for the benefit of all. An education that balances the open-mindedness of abstract knowledge with hands-on intelligence and tangible creativity; one, finally, that reconnects children with the nature to which they will always owe their survival, which awakens an awareness within them of the beauty of life and their responsibility toward it. All this is essential for raising consciousness.

> "The earth must be honored so that trees and plants may bloom, animals who eat its food thrive, and mankind live."
>
> PIERRE RABHI

3. Les Amanins: creation of an ecological, educational and solidarity-based site*

The Amanins project arose from a meeting in 2003 between Pierre Rabhi and Michel Valentin. The latter, a highly successful businessman, was in the process of reassessing the relevance of the current model. For both men, the ongoing crisis facing all humanity is not inevitable. We still have enough available resources, knowledge and expertise, financial means, and the full force of our creative powers to shift our destiny in a positive direction. With the creation of an agroecological center, the team at Les Amanins wants to promote a practical, everyday ecology, with a priority on the relationship to oneself, to others, and to nature.

Les Amanins:

An unspoiled 136-acre site located in the Drôme Valley in southeastern France, organized around an agroecological farm.

Colibri, an alternative school where children experience the direct link between knowledge and real life. They are in contact with nature and are taught to be aware of ecological issues, and learn to live together in a cooperative way.

A site for experimentation, agroecological demonstrations, and protection of biodiversity: self-generated energy (solar panels, wind power, wood stoves), entirely green buildings, phyto-purfication system for wastewater. An environmentally friendly food production zone that provides healthy produce. Most of the food is produced, transformed, and consumed on site.

* The various institutions are presented in alphabetical order.

It is a place of exchanges, training, and transmission of knowledge and expertise. It hosts visitors throughout the year for short-term or long-term stays (family visits, introduction classes, seminars, etc.).

For more information: www.lesamanins.com
Address: Les Amanins, agroecology study center
26400 La Roche-sur-Grâne
Email: info@lesamanins.com

4. Colibris: a platform for meetings and exchanges

> *One day, so the legend goes, there was a huge forest fire. All the animals were terrified, paralyzed with fear, helplessly watching the unfolding disaster.*
>
> *Alone, a tiny hummingbird was busy, fetching a few drops of water in its beak to throw on the flames.*
>
> *After a while, a grumpy armadillo, annoyed by this useless effort, cried out: "Hummingbird! Don't be a fool. You're not going to put out the fire with this drops of water!"*
>
> *To which the hummingbird replied: "That may be, but I'm doing my part."*

Pierre Rabhi and a few colleagues launched Colibris in 2007, to promote the emergence and development of new societal models based on autonomy, ecology, and a humanistic approach. Its goal is to contribute to the construction of a society based on happiness rather than the desire to "acquire." Colibris is a platform of meetings and exchanges for everyone who wants to take action, for those who are seeking tangible solutions, and developing alternatives. Colibris has elaborated the following method to help collectives of people who want to reclaim control of their destinies on their land.

Get inspired

Colibris is shaping the society of the future and exploring the latest ecological and citizen initiatives that contribute to the creation of this society through the following proposals:

– Campaigns of citizen mobilizations: Transforming our land: coming together to take action on our land / The Colibris (R)Evolution / The Oasis Project;

– "Domaine du Possible" series: books co-published with Actes Sud with the aim of creating a link between the critical findings of scientific investigation and original, practical solutions.

– *Kaizen*, a bimonthly magazine of citizen initiatives that are changing the world on step at a time;

– Documentaries: *Think Global, Act Rural* by Coline Serreau, *Au nom de la Terre* by Marie-Dominique Dhelsing, *En quête de sens* by Nathanaël Coste and Marc de la Ménardière, and *Tomorrow* by Cyril Dion and Mélanie Laurent.

Join

The Colibris movement is above all a network of local collectives throughout France, aimed at giving citizens the means to take concrete action in their territories:

– 55 groups of volunteers communicate the movement's initiatives throughout France while creating their own projects: establishing schools, local currencies, urban vegetable gardens, etc.:

– Social networks for meetings, exchanges, and mutual assistance among Colibris members;

– Directory of Colibris members: to easily find where to eat organic, local, and seasonal food, how to build a more ecological home, find or create an AMAP (Associations pour le maintien d'une agriculture paysanne, or Associations for Community-Supported Agriculture), a locally based model of agriculture and food distribution.

Support

The Oasis Project: the Colibris movement supports the creation of living spaces and resources within a building, a street, a neighborhood, a village–wherever it can! The movement calls on all citizens and elected officials to "work together" and mobilize to create new oases of mutual assistance and solidarity, and to support project implementers in the creation of their oases. More than 100 of these sites already exist in France. The goal of the project is to create one hundred additional oases within the next ten years.

University of Colibris members
The Colibris movement has launched an online university and offers free online classes to facilitate individual development and the construction of ecological projects.

The first MOOC[1] training program, "Create Your Oasis," began in January 2016. This training offers support to future initiatives, specifically financial and legal models for their projects, along with assistance in governance, planning, and ecological content.

"Colibris Project" support platform
You have a project? You need financing, volunteers, expertise, or to borrow equipment? Share your needs on the "Colibris Project" platform and receive support from the entire community.

For more information: www.colibris-lemouvement.org
Address: Mouvement Colibris, 18-20, rue Euryale Dehaynin 75019 Paris
Tel: +33 (0)1 42 15 50 17
Email: info@colibris-lemouvement.org

[1]. A MOOC (Massive Open Online Course) is an online course open to all, including high-quality teaching videos, exercises, a platform for exchanges among participants, etc.

5. The ferme des enfants and the Hameau des Buis: building the future with a respect for life

Since 1999, the Ferme des Enfants has been using the Montessori method on a farm for preschool, elementary and middle-school children. Families can opt for an alternative teaching approach that matches their dreams for their children's education. The school teaches about:
 – life: acquisition of essential knowledge and expertise, self-knowledge and fostering awareness;
 – peace: implementation of children's councils, experimentation with a democratic system, nonviolent communication, listening, managing emotions, etc.;
 – ecology: discovery and knowledge of the natural environment, its potential, its diversity, respectful management of resources, ecological practices, waste sorting, and recycling, etc.;
 – society: social education through encounters with artists, professionals, scientists, travelers, living together with retired people.

In 2004, the school opened up to a wider public with the creation of the Hameau des Buis, a genuine oasis of life and an experimental laboratory working for the general public interest. An "ecological, educational, and intergenerational living space" was created on 2.5 acres of constructible land, with a traditional stone farmhouse, along with 15 acres of farmland. The goal:
 – an alternative approach to living: buildings that respect the land and the trees, constructed with natural materials that offer high energy efficiency and optimal water management;
 – to consume differently: by sharing funds, equipment, and tools; a return to earlier practices, knowledge, and expertise; setting up organic, ethical, and local food networks;

– to eat differently: by producing food using agroecological methods, diversifying food production, actively maintaining biodiversity, selling agricultural produce locally;
– to move around differently: by limiting travel through autonomy, group orders and deliveries, carpooling, etc.

The Hameau des Buis is open for regular visits.

For more information: www.la-ferme-des-enfants.com
Address: Le Hameau des Buis / La Ferme des Enfants
07230 Lablachère
Tel: +33 (0)4 75 35 09 97
Email: ecole@la-ferme-des-enfants.com

6. The Solan Monastery: combining liturgy and farming

By celebrating the natural world as a creation and gift from God, the fifteen nuns (with seven different nationalities) at the Solan Monastery were among the first to adopt agroecology. From the start, when they moved to the Gard département in 1992, the community decided not to "abandon the earth," but to restore it, through harmony and fertility. The desire to combine the church liturgy with farming the land was a deeply felt conviction. Their meeting with Pierre Rabhi was providential, as it opened their horizons and offered them a tangible path to achieving their goal. Today, they pursue multiple activities:
– an agroecological kitchen garden, which provides them–as well as all those who come to the monastery for an exchange or spiritual assistance–with most of their vegetables;
– an exemplary program for protecting the property's biodiversity;

– production and sale of organic wine (approximately 30,000 bottles per year; certain vintages have acquired considerable recognition).

Through this experience, Pierre Rabhi met the orthodox patriarch of Romania, which led to the development of an extensive agroecological program throughout all of that country's monasteries, with the goal of producing high-quality food for hundreds of thousands of people.

An experience of the "power of restraint"

> Our lives are governed by a concern for moderation, restraint, and vigilance. This implies temperance and self-control, self-limits, voluntarily restricting our patterns of food consumption and of natural resources. These restrictions are the path to the great joy that fills our lives, a joy derived from the liberation–gradual, laborious, and never complete–from our selfish pursuit of pleasure.
>
> As we renounce these selfish tendencies, we become able to perceive the harmony of creation and feel a sense of wonder at the beauty of the universe.
>
> If in our innermost beings we are motivated by love, good choices arise spontaneously and we become unified. It is then that renunciation becomes the path to fulfillment, and that restraint leads to happiness, in the full sense of the term.
>
> The nuns of Solan

For more information: www.monasteredesolan.com
Address: Monastère de Solan, 30330 La Bastide-d'Engras
Tel: +33 (0)4 66 82 94 25

7. Terre & Humanisme: transmitting agroecology here and elsewhere ...

Launched in 1994 by Pierre Rabhi, the association Terre & Humanisme owes its name to the importance of the link between humankind and Mother Earth. There is no ecology without solidarity.

Agroecology is a global alternative that combines farming practices with an ethical life. Given the brutal assessments of a depleted earth, it offers natural solutions to regenerate it, with a respect for all living organisms, humans included. It incorporates social, health, economic, and environmental aspects.

From the Mas de Beaulieu, a site the promotes experimentation, demonstrations, and production in the southern Ardèche, Terre & Humanisme practices and transmits the principles of agroecology: hosting volunteers, training for the public at large (vegetable gardens, cooking, apiculture), training for instructors, etc. It also conducts programs abroad, which is a major part of its activities. It helps to promote autonomy and food independence among African villages through local partnerships and training for instructors.

From an ecological standpoint: preservation and regeneration of soil, addition of humus to maintain fertility, optimization of water use, respect and preservation of biodiversity, combat soil erosion and desertification on arid land.

From an economic standpoint: considerable reduction in production costs due to the irrelevance of chemical additives–an alternative suited to the precarious livelihoods of people living in the southern hemisphere; relocalization of the economy by encouraging the use of local resources, which then reduces the transportation that adds to energy dependence and destroys natural environments.

From a social standpoint: food autonomy for individuals and local collectives while maintaining bartering systems, which bolster friendly relationships and an open society; this reduces the flow of migrants and the spread of poverty; quantitative production of high-quality food, a factor of good health.

For more information: www.terre-humanisme.org
Address: Terre & Humanisme, mas de Beaulieu, BP 19
07230 Lablachère
Tel: +33 (0)4 75 36 64 01
Email: infos@terre-humanisme.org

8. Outreach and prospects for the future

> Food health and security is understood to be a situation that is ensured by communities themselves on their own land, and not through artificial aid that makes certain countries dependent on unpredictable charitable assistance, which goes against the dignity of upright, responsible human beings... We have also seen that food produced using agroecological practices reduces the number of illnesses that now affect the world's population.
>
> PIERRE RABHI

Since 1981, Pierre Rabhi has been teaching agroecology in a certain number of national structures and, since the creation and management of the Gorom-Gorom training center in Burkina Faso in 1984, he has been transmitting his expertise in different regions of the world, seeking to return food autonomy to local populations. Since its creation in 1994, Terre & Humanisme France has been involved in these international initiatives.

With the exception of assistance required to respond to natural cataclysms, our goal is to eliminate humanitarian aid, to be replaced by a humanistic approach based on a concern for people and for nature, to which we all owe our lives and our survival. The work with the poorest populations must not be shaped by a desire to help, but by a concern to respond to the demands of communities, in accordance with the essential needs that they themselves have defined. It is not about imposing a clichéd vision of life and well-being, modeled after the Western experience, which is itself in crisis. The specific aspects of each situation must be factored in for mutual enrichment with a respect for traditions, cultures and lifestyles.

International programs

For many years, programs promoting the transmission of agroecological expertise and knowledge have been undertaken successfully in Mali, Senegal, Tunisia, Burkina Faso, and Cameroon, among others, to improve the food autonomy of local populations, to help them save their food-producing heritage, to fight desertification, and to renew natural environments in a respectful way.

In 2005, Terre & Humanisme Morocco was created, four years after Pierre Rabhi participated in the international conference "Chemins d'Alliance entre Féminin d'Orient et d'Occident," organized by the association ESPOD. Since then, agroecology training sessions have been conducted on pilot sites in Morocco, such as the Jnane Lakbir farm in Dar Bouazza, near Casablanca, and the farm in the village of Kermet Ben Salem, near Meknès. A training center, the Carrefour International des Initiatives Agroécologiques, was inaugurated in spring of 2015 near Marrakech. It provides local, national, and international training in agroecology to small farmers.

Encouraging the expansion of agroecology throughout the world

Given the uncertainty of oil and gas energy, on which modern agricultural production depends more than ever, agroecology is viewed by a growing number of stakeholders as an inevitable alternative. The message that we promote and live by everyday through the different structures described above is reaching an ever-increasing public; it is being heard and considered seriously by the various elements of our society. To support the emergence of a new societal model based on the principle of living organisms and on ensuring the food health, security, and autonomy of all populations, our valuable experience must be encouraged and transmitted to the largest number of people in both the northern and southern hemispheres.

The Fondation Pierre Rabhi was created in 2010 to meet the quasi-exponential growth in requests. The Pierre Rabhi Endowment Fund (Fonds de Dotation Pierre Rabhi) replaced this foundation in 2013; its goal is to help promote and develop agroecology and its implementation through the creation of ecological, pedagogical, and intergenerational places to live.

If we want to ensure the sustainability and advancement of the human species on the planet, we must construct new societal models that place the human being and nature at the center of our priorities. Above all, this sustainable society must feed its population in a healthy manner, preserve and regenerate the natural environment, and reconnect people with nature, with the utmost concern for the fate of future generations.

Designed by
Atelier Graphique Actes Sud
and Printed in July 2017
by Normandie Roto Impression s.a.s.
61250 Lonrai
N° 1701816
on paper made of wood from
sustainably managed forests
for Actes Sud
Le Méjan
Place Nina-Berberova
13200 Arles.

Legal deposit, first edition: October 2017
(Printed in France)